Solving Skills Shortages

THE INDUSTRIAL SOCIETY

The Industrial Society stands for changing people's lives. In nearly eighty years of business, the Society has a unique record of transforming organisations by unlocking the potential of their people, bringing unswerving commitment to best practice and tempered by a mission to listen and learn from experience.

The Industrial Society's clear vision of ethics, excellence and learning at work has never been more important. Over 10,000 organisations, including most of the companies that are household names, benefit from corporate Society membership.

The Society works with these, and non-member organisations, in a variety of ways – consultancy, management and skills training, in-house and public courses, information services and multi-media publishing. All this with the single vision – to unlock the potential of people and organisations by promoting ethical standards, excellence and learning at work.

If you would like to know more about the Industrial Society please contact us.

The Industrial Society
48 Bryanston Square
London
W1H 7LN
Telephone 0171 262 2401

The Industrial Society is a Registered Charity No. 290003

Solving Skills Shortages

HOW TO RECRUIT AND RETAIN SKILLED PEOPLE

Hilton Catt & Patricia Scudamore

KOGAN
PAGE

YOURS TO HAVE AND TO HOLD
BUT NOT TO COPY

The publication you are reading is protected by copyright law. This means that the publisher could take you and your employer to court and claim heavy legal damages if you make unauthorised photocopies from these pages. Photocopying copyright material without permission is no different from stealing a magazine from a newsagent, only it doesn't seem like theft.

The Copyright Licensing Agency (CLA) is an organisation which issues licences to bring photocopying within the law. It has designed licensing services to cover all kinds of special needs in business, education and government.

If you take photocopies from books, magazines and periodicals at work your employer should be licensed with CLA. Make sure you are protected by a photocopying licence.

The Copyright Licensing Agency Limited, 90 Tottenham Court Road, London, W1P 0LP. Tel: 0171 436 5931. Fax: 0171 436 3986.

First published in 1997

Apart from any fair dealing for the purposes of research or private study, or criticism or review, as permitted under the Copyright, Designs and Patents Act, 1988, this publication may only be reproduced, stored or transmitted, in any form or by any means, with the prior permission in writing of the publishers, or in the case of reprographic reproduction in accordance with the terms and licences issued by the CLA. Enquiries concerning reproduction outside those terms should be sent to the publishers at the undermentioned address:

Kogan Page Limited
120 Pentonville Road
London N1 9JN

© Hilton Catt and Patricia Scudamore, 1997

The right of Hilton Catt and Patricia Scudamore to be identified as authors of this work has been asserted by them in accordance with the Copyright, Designs and Patents Act 1988.

British Library Cataloguing in Publication Data

A CIP record for this book is available from the British Library.

ISBN 0 7494 2055 3

Phototypeset by Intype London Ltd
Printed in England by Clays Ltd, St Ives plc

Contents

Introduction

This book is based on a series of seminars we ran a few years ago when the problem of skills shortages began to surface, notably in manufacturing industry.

There are two facets to skills shortages:

- *retention difficulties* – companies finding it hard to hang onto the skilled workers they've got.

- *recruitment difficulties* – inability to attract new people (either additional or replacements).

Recruitment difficulties break down into two sorts:

- sourcing difficulties (too few or no applicants);

- conversion difficulties (failing to turn applicants into starters).

We have written this book with practising managers and Human Resources specialists in mind – indeed anyone who is likely to find themselves at the sharp end of skills shortages and having to solve them. The accent throughout is on giving practical advice which readers can use, in the sense that:

- everything has been tried in the field. We specialise in skilled recruitment and it is the sum total of our experience over a number of years;

- it won't cost an arm and a leg to use. Indeed – because of the large amounts of cash that organisations with skills shortages tend to splash out on advertising and consultants' fees, we can feel justified in saying to most users: 'this is going to save you money'.

Among the key issues we will be dealing with are:

- how skilled people view the job market;
- what companies can do to stop skilled people leaving;
- how best to recruit skilled people: what works and what doesn't;
- why some jobs attract few applicants;
- how companies can get a better response to their recruitment advertising;
- how to use resources to best effect and thereby save time and money;
- how cheap available technology can help companies become better at recruiting people with scarce skills.

What do we mean by skilled people?

We use the term to describe people with hands-on skills, people who perform manual tasks which require training – usually in the form of an apprenticeship or its equivalent. In most cases the training given would be supported by appropriate further education such as a City & Guilds qualification. The skills acquired would then be subject to development by experience. A fully skilled person is therefore someone who has undergone several years of training, education and job experience.

There are skilled people in every walk of life. The engineering industry employs skilled people in large numbers. So does the building trade. There are skilled people in public utilities and local authorities. Even banks, insurance companies, large stores and hotels use skilled people to look after their premises and facilities.

1

Reasons for Skills Shortages

UNDERSTANDING THE PROBLEM

How do we deal with skills shortages?

Before we can begin to address this problem, we need first to ask the question, why do skills shortages exist? This chapter highlights briefly the answers to such a fundamental question.

The pool of skilled people in this country is shrinking. Ask any human resources manager why and he or she will probably offer you one of two explanations:

1. The decline in skills training since the 1970s – particularly the traditional apprenticeship.

2. The poor uptake of what training places *are* available, reflecting perhaps a changed view of skilled manual employment among today's school leavers ('not what we want').

To these commonly stated reasons for the shrinking pool we would add a third. With every recession (and we have had two whoppers in the last fifteen years) there are a certain number of skilled people who quit their trades. 'Fed up with being made redundant' is the frequently stated reason. They go on to being jobbing gardeners, shopkeepers, postmen, caretakers, all sorts of things, and few ever come back because, being on the whole tenacious and capable people, they tend to make a success of their new careers. No-one knows with any accuracy just how many skilled people have been lost from the workforce in this way but our guess is that it is substantial.

There is an interesting corollary to the decline in new entrants to skilled occupations. The skilled workforce is ageing.

For a number of years we have run a recruitment business in the West Midlands which specialises in skilled people as well as people in technical occupations such as design and quality engineers. Every year that goes by we have seen the people we are dealing with (the candidates) getting older and older. In 1990 the average age of skilled candidate we had on file was around 39. Today (1996) this average is more like 46/47. Skilled people under 30 are becoming very scarce indeed.

We will have more to say about this ageing factor as we go on.

THE MARKET FOR SKILLED PEOPLE: SUPPLY AND DEMAND

In looking at recruitment and retention issues the first hard fact for all of us to swallow is that in times of economic buoyancy there are never going to be enough skilled people to go around. Everyone will be trying to take a bigger and bigger bite out of a cake which is slowly getting smaller in size.

One of the further problems with the supply of skilled people is its inelasticity. You don't suddenly turn on the tap and increase the numbers of skilled people on the market by stepping up the investment in training. It all takes too long. Trade booms can come and go in less time than it takes to bring a skilled worker on stream. Training is a long-term answer. It doesn't solve today's problems.

But that's not all. Every market has two sides to it – a buyer and a seller, a supply and a demand. Up until now we have been looking at the supply side of the skilled labour market, the people themselves. But this doesn't give us the full picture because part of the problem of skills shortages lies with employers – what they do and changes in what they want.

EMPLOYERS WHO CONTRIBUTE TO SKILLS SHORTAGES

To see how employers can contribute to skills shortages let us take an example. In a typical modern manufacturing business, maintenance personnel no longer work within strictly demarcated lines of skill as they did years ago. Nowadays they are expected to be 'multi-skilled' – a term used to indicate how they must be capable of diagnosing and rectifying both mechanical and electrical faults as well as delving into hydraulics, pneumatics and all sorts of other things. The old fashioned single discipline mechanical or electrical fitter doesn't fit into this picture. The modern specification is thus much tighter and this of course means that fewer and fewer candidates are going to be suitable. The scarcity factor increases.

Technology has contributed to skills shortages too. If we stick to our example of maintenance personnel in a modern manufacturing environment we see employers these days looking for people who are little short of Mr Black Boxes – people who can fault-find and problem solve on all manner of sophisticated computerised machinery. In some cases this introduces a preference for younger candidates – people who will be seen as having a better appreciation of new technology – which in turn brings employers face to face with the acute shortage of skilled people in the under 30 age bracket.

SUMMARY

Skills shortages are here to stay and will become more acute every time we hit a boom. Keeping your slice of the skills cake intact calls for new ideas in retention and recruitment. Read on . . .

2

Living with Skills Shortages

HOW EMPLOYERS WITH SKILLS SHORTAGES MANAGE

Stickley & Stopgap Limited is a precision engineering business employing around 250 people. The order book has improved significantly in the last few months but the company is dogged by chronic skills shortages. There are currently six vacancies for skilled machinists of various types.

Several advertisements in the local evening paper have yielded absolutely nothing and the Job Centre has been unable to come up with any suitable candidates. The company is now at the stage where it is having to turn work away. The managing director's view is that further attempts at recruiting skilled people will be a waste of time and money. The only answer, it seems to him, is putting up the rates of pay to attract applicants but he is reluctant to do this because much of the work is competitively priced.

Firms who can't recruit skilled people tend to attribute their lack of success to one of three reasons:

- no suitable applicants exist (they are simply not there);
- 'we are in a bad area';
- 'we don't pay enough and we can't afford to pay more'.

The signal to these firms is to give up and where they go from there depends very much on them.

Turning away customers is one not very satisfactory approach to living with skills shortages but there are others which have equal doses of venom in their tails:

- **Putting work out:** eg to the subcontract trade. The main snag here is the cost. In some cases this can be astronomical.

- **Stepping up overtime:** Again there is a price to pay, this time in terms of wage costs (overtime payments at premium rates). Also viewed as long-term arrangements, excessive hours tend to be self defeating. Productivity falls, the money associated with overtime starts to rank in people's expectations (making it hard to take away), bills on heat, light, power and factory services go up – and so on.

- **Rearranging shift patterns:** (where shifts are worked) eg if three fitters provide round-the-clock maintenance cover by working eight-hour shifts (6am to 2pm/2pm to 10pm/10pm to 6am) and one leaves then the remaining two can continue to provide cover by working 12-hour shifts (6am to 6pm/6pm to 6am). The implications here are much the same as working more overtime. Also, what happens if another fitter leaves?

- **Bringing in temps:** In times of skills shortages asking agencies to find skilled temps probably has even less chance of success than recruiting permanent staff. Temps are expensive and not always up to scratch. Also agencies' ideas on acceptable skill levels are not always in tune with those of their clients. It is interesting to note how many agencies put disclaimers in their terms of business to clear them of any responsibility for damages their temps might cause. Is this a mark of their confidence in the kind of people they supply?

The other aspect to living with skills shortages is just how long some firms are prepared to run with the problem. We come across cases where vacancies have existed for months and occasionally years.

SUMMARY

Trying to sidestep skills shortages rarely works. Face up to the problem and don't jump to hasty conclusions about your inability to retain and recruit skilled people.

3

Stopping Skilled People Leaving: Seeking Reasons for Retention Difficulties

INTERPRETING LABOUR TURNOVER

A sudden upsurge in labour turnover shouldn't necessarily be read as a retention crisis. For example, an increase in leavers at the end of a period of recession is to some extent inevitable and nowhere more so than with the skilled sector. These, after all, will be the people most sought after on the outside labour market.

Two factors tend to explain these post-recessionary blips:

- Few employment opportunities in the preceding period, meaning few leavers (lower than normal turnover) which produces a buildup of people who are looking to move on. In other words what you could be witnessing is three years of normal turnover compressed into six months.

- During recessions people, particularly unemployed people, take on jobs as stop gaps, eg jobs further from their homes than they would ideally like to travel. Such people tend to leave as soon as the job market picks up.

TERMINATION INTERVIEWS

What about termination interviews? There was a time when most professionally minded companies carried out systematic termination interviews on all their leavers to find out their reasons. Some still do.

Critics of termination interviews consider they are a complete waste of time. It's rather like trying to bolt the stable door when the horse is already in full flight, they will say. But in fairness to termination interviews, they were never designed as a platform for talking people out of leaving. The hope was, rather, that something of value could be learned from what a leaver had to say, something which might help to prevent the next person putting in his or her notice.

Undoubtedly some very useful information can be gleaned from termination interviews – like identifying bad managers or finding out what competitors for labour are paying. But in practice do leavers ever tell the truth or the whole truth? Do they use the interview instead as an opportunity to do a bit of stirring or do they tell the interviewer what he or she wants to hear? In fact, does too much depend on the skill and experience of the interviewer?

Another problem with termination interviews is the time they take. Management time in today's delayered, re-engineered and slimline industrial society is very much at a premium. Those who can remember the good old days will remember how responsibility for carrying out termination interviews usually fell on the Human Resources department. Typically it formed part and parcel of the job description of the average personnel officer. Now of course it is common to find Human Resources departments downsized or, in some cases, they've gone altogether. The time to do termination interviews and do them properly is a problem to employers.

One approach to termination interviews is to carry them out on a selective and *ad hoc* basis. For example, if the problem is retention of plastic injection moulding machine toolsetters. Answer: interview all toolsetters who leave over a period of, say, six months and see what conclusions you draw. Because the interviews are targeted and for a fixed period only, the workload won't be quite so prohibitive.

One problem with termination interviews in the modern environment is that they frequently fall onto the shoulders of line managers. Here the dangers are:

- the leaver may not be quite so forthcoming when talking to the boss;

- line managers may filter out anything that smacks of criticism of themselves;

- line managers frequently have axes to grind. For instance, they may be sympathetic to the view that their subordinates are underpaid. Consciously or not, questions can be structured to tempt out replies which support the manager's arguments.

THE ORGANIC NATURE OF RETENTION DIFFICULTIES

If you take out the rogue manager – of which, sorry to say, there has been a bit of a glut in recent years – most real retention difficulties we come across are organic in nature, by which we mean they are structural, complex and long term – if you like, a slow whittling away of the skilled workforce over a period of years. The latest research on labour turnover seems to bear out this view. Hence scuttling around looking for simplistic, off the shelf reasons for retention difficulties becomes a bit like a manic game of hunt the thimble when the thimble isn't actually there.

Yet simplistic reasons are what most companies tend to latch on to, and from these simplistic reasons they start to think out all sorts of equally simplistic solutions which, when applied, don't work.

XYZ Limited is in the business of providing on-site maintenance services to owners of commercial premises. XYZ employs a team of field service engineers and each of these engineers has a company van. Over a period of six months a number of engineers leave. XYZ don't do termination interviews as a matter of course but the feedback they pick up is that leavers are going to jobs which provide estate cars rather than vans. XYZ react by announcing that they too will be providing estate cars in future (as and when the vans come up for replacement). This news is greeted warmly by the service engineers (as one would expect) and XYZ think they have cracked their retention problem. However the stream of leavers continues.

XYZ's experience is fairly typical.

SUMMARY

Don't bother with termination interviews unless you can do them properly. Don't focus on simplistic reasons for labour turnover either. View retention difficulties as organic and 'curable' only in the long term and with a fair degree of management determination. Pay particular attention to our chapter on training (Chapter 15).

4

Stopping Skilled People Leaving: Retention Devices

There are some companies who have very little turnover of people, including skilled grades, and often you find that these are not necessarily companies who pay the highest rates or dole out the biggest perks. True, in a few cases they are companies in the enviable position of having little or no competition for the labour they employ – for example companies in isolated geographical locations. Yet it has to be said that these firms with low turnover are for the most part normal run-of-the-mill operations making normal run-of-the-mill products or providing normal run-of-the-mill services and doing these things in normal run-of-the-mill places.

So what big secrets do they have?

What binds a lot of these firms together is that somehow they have managed to instil a spirit of 'feel good' in their employees; the feeling they are being looked after and that they belong to something worth belonging to, something they would never willingly want to leave. Some people might describe such firms not too politely as paternalistic and maybe they are right, but perhaps, in the game of retention, whether we like it or not paternalistic works.

But paternalism – or a caring style of management as we prefer to call it – is only half the story. Getting to the level where retention ceases to be an issue is usually the result of painstakingly good management practice over many years. Sadly, the circumstances in which most companies have had to operate in recent times have not been conducive to the growth of 'feelgood' factors. Lay-offs and redundancies have taken their toll. Delayerings and restructurings have played havoc with people's careers. Feelgood is also about having confidence in management and in this context continuity of management is important. It is hard to have confidence in a management which keeps changing and in some companies tenure of management positions has been notoriously short. Instances of firms where there have been three managing directors in the space of eighteen months are not that uncommon these days.

RESTORING THE 'FEELGOOD' FACTOR

Putting the feelgood factor back into a business is no easy task. It is only achievable:

- with a great deal of management effort and determination;

- over a long period of time.

Even so, there are no guarantees that the feelgood factor will return. However, because there is no way of putting skills' retention difficulties on hold, most companies with turnover problems tend to resort to what we describe as 'retention devices'. We want to look at retention devices in more detail now but it is important that from the outset you view them as the painkillers rather than the cures.

BUYING LEAVERS OFF AND PERKS AS RETENTION DEVICES

Money is at the root of most moves to stop skilled people leaving, money in the form of:

- *buy-offs* – matching or improving on whatever leavers have been offered;

- *selective pay increases* – identifying high turnover groups and targeting them with rises.

Money is the blunt instrument of retention and recruitment technology. There is no doubt that in most cases it works but the problem for most larger companies is that they are not free to engineer buy-offs or selective pay increases without:

- going to the top of the tree for approval (which takes time);
- creating anomalies and upsetting the balance of the pay structure (differentials);
- with buy-offs, running the risk of encouraging others to chance their arm and put their notice in too.

Pay is an emotive and complex subject. We will be looking at pay in more detail in the next chapter.

Once upon a time compulsory membership of the pension scheme was seen as one of the best ways of encouraging staff to stay – particularly if leavers were seen to get raw deals in the form of paltry frozen pensions. Recent pensions legislation has done much to take away this particular retention lever with many employees opting instead for completely portable personal pensions or exercising their right not to join the pension scheme at all. And, let's face it, the greater feeling of insecurity about jobs hasn't helped. Not many people really rate their chances of seeing out their time and picking up their pension at 65.

Forfeiting the gold watch after 25 years' service may no longer disincline many people towards leaving but loss of benefits like free medical plans, cheap personal loans and – in the case of public companies – SAYE share option schemes can and do exercise powerful retaining influences, particularly where competitors for labour can't or don't offer the same thing.

But increasingly, these days, companies with retention problems are looking at other, more exotic methods of making life difficult for those who choose to go shopping round the job market and two of these are worth mentioning in the context of skilled employment.

CONTRACTUAL RESTRAINTS

Restraints are devices you tend to associate with management contracts – or with those of people like salesmen. A restraint is any term in a contract which puts restrictions on what employees can do after they leave – such as work for competitors.

On the whole Human Resources practitioners take a jaundiced view of contractual restraints. They see them as unsatisfactory and largely unenforceable particularly where the restraint interferes with the individual's right to earn a living – and, when it comes to it, who in their right minds would try to enforce a contractual restraint anyway?

In our experience restraints are used (a) rarely and (b) very selectively in the field of skilled employment. An example, fairly typical, is the highly specialised contract toolmaking business seeking to prevent a top toolmaker going off to work for the competition and taking with him know-how and customer contacts. The restraint is usually part of a deal struck with an employee such as this which might have other features such as a big pay rise, staff status or, in some cases, access to a company vehicle – in other words conditions which would not be extended to everyone on the payroll.

Do restraints on skilled people work? The feedback from the field is that they can, but not in the way most people expect. In the real world of employment the most significant thing about a restraint in someone's contract is that it acts as a deterrent to a potential recruiter, particularly if the potential recruiter happens to be a small business. The prospect of injunctions flying round doesn't appeal one little bit to the average owner of a small business. The vibes about candidates subject to restraints are to leave them well alone. This will of course be possible if an acceptable alternative (and unrestrained) candidate exists.

The off-putting effect of restraints presumes of course that the recruiter is aware of their existence and since few recruiters of skilled labour are attuned to asking questions about contractual restraints as part of their interview patter this is not necessarily a foregone conclusion. Awareness of restraints will depend to a large extent on whether the candidate volunteers the information or not.

Verdict on restraint clauses? Probably not what most larger companies would want to get involved in.

EXTENDING NOTICE PERIODS

This is the device of putting groups of skilled employees on longer periods of notice, eg one month instead of the usual one week.

Companies who have gone along this particular route normally did so in the first place because they saw it as a way of giving themselves extra time for finding replacements for skilled people who leave. The extra time is needed because:

- experience shows finding replacements is difficult;

- with a bit of luck it might give the leaver/new starter an overlapping handover period.

Extended notice periods can, however, act as quite useful retention devices. They function in two ways:

- They give the leaver more time to reflect on his/her decision. They allow time for second thoughts to creep in and sometimes leavers change their minds while working out long notice periods (the 'cold feet' effect).

- More importantly, rather like restraint clauses, long notice periods are a definite deterrent to recruiters. Recruiters in the skilled market are usually people in a hurry. They don't tend to want to wait round for someone on a month or three months' notice, particularly if – once again – acceptable alternative candidates exist who can start the following week.

Are there any downsides for the employer to putting skilled categories on long periods of notice?

Here are some of the answers practitioners have given us over the years:

- It doesn't pay to frustrate people who want to leave. It's best that they go.

- People won't in any case work out long periods of notice. Interestingly, though, the anecdotal evidence of people cutting notice periods short is contradictory. For what it's worth, we have placed many hundreds of skilled people in jobs over the years and never once experienced a candidate cutting an extended notice period short. This includes candidates on three months' notice.

- Notice periods cut both ways. You can't extend notice one way (employee to employer) without doing it the other way too (employer to employee). This means it will cost you in payments in lieu of notice if you have to shed a number of people in a hurry or if short service people prove unsatisfactory.

This last objection smacks a bit of nitpicking and failing to see the bigger issues but, if potential in lieu payments are a concern to anyone, then they may be interested to learn what a couple of companies we are acquainted with did when it came to extending notice periods for their skilled people. These companies used as a basis the statutory employer to employee notice periods (ie one week per year of service up to a maximum of twelve weeks for those with twelve years service or more) and extended them to the contractual employee to employer requirement. This meant that the period of notice both ways is:

- always the same

- goes up with service.

The benefits both of these companies see in this arrangement are:

- it overcomes the pay in lieu of notice problem and enables them to dispose of short service people inexpensively;

- the retention pressure is put on the people you most want to retain, ie the longer serving/most experienced;

- because the same notice periods are binding on both employer and employee, the arrangement is regarded as acceptable and fair, ie few problems were experienced in implementation.

Verdict on extended notice periods? Having key people on a week's notice is probably not a good idea anyway.

Tales from the front line

A company we came across a few years ago hit on the ingenious idea of knocking half day holidays on the head. This, they reckoned, was how most of their employees managed to get to attend job interviews.

Is there anything else companies can do to combat growing turnover of staff in skilled areas?

RE-EMPLOYING EX-STAFF

It is interesting to note that about 40 per cent of skilled people we interview are people who have taken a new job in the fairly recent past (ie the last twelve months) and who now feel they made a bad move. They were misled, they say, meaning the job was misrepresented – either they were given duff information at the interview or promises were made to them which never materialised.

A lot of the focus on leavers goes into the period just after they hand in their notice (eg termination interviews). Very few companies in our experience bother to contact leavers two to three months after they have left. Yet, if there is disillusionment with the new job, this is when it will be starting to set in.

Some leavers will return, cap in hand, and ask if their old job is still open but they are probably a minority. Pride is a very strong emotion and for most of us it is far, far easier just to go back out on the job market and see what else we can find.

Systematically recontacting leavers a few months after they have gone (those you want back of course) can be a very worthwhile exercise. From the company's point of view:

- it's the cost of a telephone call;

- it could save the time and expense of recruiting replacements;

- it's someone who can do the job;

- if it works out it has a sobering effect on any others who may be contemplating leaving (in fact, a very good retention device in itself!).

By asking, the company is making it easier for the ex-employee to come back. The ice is broken and there is no feeling of having eaten humble pie.

SUMMARY
Don't expect retention devices to perform miracles for you. Use them only if you think they are (a) appropriate and (b) won't create more problems than they solve. Recontacting leavers is certainly worth trying.

5

Are You Paying Enough?

PAY PARANOIA

This is the question which bothers all employers of skilled labour. How competitive are we? How exposed are we to the attentions of predators?

Gripnuts Limited is in the business of making special purpose fasteners which they supply to the construction industry. The company's markets have been very depressed in the last four to five years but things have started to pick up recently, thanks mainly to a spate of export orders.

Because Gripnuts value the skills and experience of their workforce they fought their way through the lean times with very few redundancies. Pay rises, however, were minimal and for two consecutive years there have been no pay rises at all.

In the top echelon of their production labour, Gripnuts have a team of skilled people who set cold forging machines. In recent months four of these people have left for better paid jobs and Gripnuts have been unable to replace them. Advertisements in the local evening paper have brought in a poor response (the people who applied did not have the necessary experience) and Gripnuts are now getting concerned. Chief among these concerns is the feeling they might be out of step with the going rate in the area for cold forging setters and, to lend weight to this impression, several of the senior setters have been saying that they can easily get another £2 an hour by shopping round. The management of Gripnuts are now fearful that a number of these key setters may suddenly vote with their feet and go – then where will the company be?

Pay paranoia describes the condition where firms start to think that everyone else or almost everyone else is paying more than they do and how, when it comes to rates they must be somewhere near the bottom of the heap. There are a lot of firms suffering from pay paranoia. They can't all be right, can they?

SOURCES OF INFORMATION ON PAY COMPETITIVENESS

First of all, how do you actually check out where you stand in the pay stakes in your area? There are several traditional ways of doing this which we can break down under two main headings: the formal and the informal.

- *Formal methods* include professionally produced pay surveys and information networked in from other employers (eg the Human Resources departments of certain companies in a given area may swap pay information with one another as a matter of course or via an employers' association).

- *Informal methods* take in feedback from leavers (perhaps from termination interviews), feedback from employment interviews (what job candidates are earning) and local grapevines.

One of the great difficulties for employers these days is that information on levels of pay for a given trade and in a given area (formally and informally sourced) is sometimes conflicting and frequently confusing.

Tales from the Front Line

One managing director said to us a few years ago, 'Our skilled rates are always in the upper quartile of these pay surveys I buy but it still doesn't stop the b****rs leaving!'

So what's going on here?

WHATEVER HAPPENED TO THE GOING RATE?

We have seen enormous changes in patterns of employment in recent years. The recessions we had in the early 80s and again in 1990–1994 exacted a huge toll on big name companies, the large firms who were such a dominant feature of the employment scene up to the 70s. Up and down the country the big names have been diminished in size, broken up or, in some cases, ceased to exist altogether. In their place a patchwork quilt of small- to medium-sized firms has sprung up, together with a shift from traditional industries to an array of all sorts of different kinds of businesses. Thus the big foundry which closed its doors in 1982 has been knocked down to make way for an industrial estate where electronics companies sit next door to clothing manufacturers and light engineering businesses.

With this fragmentation of the employment market and the decline of collective bargaining (particularly local and national agreements) which featured in industries like engineering, the concept of a 'going rate' has all but disappeared. This is what many employers find extremely hard to grasp. What they spend so much time fishing for simply doesn't exist any more. The nice, neatly ordered world has gone where the rate for the job was determined by what the big firms in the area happened to pay.

Let's take a typical modern market situation.

PP Plastics manufactures extruded plastic sections mainly for the replacement window frame trade. It employs six people including the proprietor, Maurice Phelps, and it has been trading for the last five years. Up to now Maurice has maintained the machines himself as well as carrying out routine repairs on the intricate little extrusion dies which PP Plastics use. However, the business is expanding and Maurice realises his time would be far better spent on sales and general management. He decides therefore to recruit a toolmaker and through an acquaintance he is put in touch with George Ashworth, a toolmaker with lots of experience on maintaining extrusion dies. George pops round one evening after work. He tells Maurice he is earning £8.75 per hour with his present employer, KK Tools, and he has ten hours overtime a week guaranteed. Maurice offers him £10 and agrees to guarantee the same levels of overtime. The two of them shake hands on the deal.

KK Tools probably feel they are paying George not a bad rate and they will be surprised when he puts his notice in and tells them he has been offered better money elsewhere. They may well start to feel confused and wonder if they are paying enough.

Of course Maurice Phelps's decision to offer George £10 an hour had nothing at all to do with going rates or what the latest survey on toolmakers' pay had to say. Two factors only were weighing on his mind:

- The benefit to him personally of not having to drop everything and dash out into the works with his box of tools every time a die got damaged or a machine broke down.

- Putting enough on top of what George is earning already to make the move attractive to him. If George had been earning £7.50 an hour then no doubt Maurice would have been offering him rather less than £10.

'So what's new?' we can hear you saying. 'Haven't small firms always acted in this way?' The answer is yes, of course they have. Small firms poaching from big firms probably goes back to the Industrial Revolution and beyond. But what is different about small firms these days is that there are far more of them about. By the next century most people in the UK will be working in firms which employ less than fifty people. Hence rates of pay for people in demand are more and more likely to be determined by the kind of one-on-one bargaining which went on between Maurice and George – and this clearly poses problems for larger employers who are less free to proceed in the same way.

We now return to Gripnuts who, you will remember, lost four key setters in a short period and failed to replace them. Not unnaturally this suggested to Gripnuts that they could have a pay problem. The fact they had just gone through a period of low to nil pay increases tended to reinforce the view that lack of pay competitiveness was at the root of their recruitment and retention difficulties.

In the end Gripnuts bit the bullet and in the guise of a bit of bogus job evaluation hiked up the rates for their skilled setters by about 90p an hour. No more setters left and Gripnuts felt they had achieved at least something. The disappointment, however, was in recruitment. Even with better rates the vacancies still proved very hard to fill.

The interesting thing about Gripnuts (and why we have included them) is that they exemplify companies whose real problems have nothing to do with pay.

WHEN INCREASING PAY WON'T HELP

Accepting that lack of pay competitiveness is a common enough reason for firms not being able to recruit, it is nevertheless very easy to pick up false readings. False readings can arise because:

- the wrong recruiting methods are being used and this – rather than pay – is why no-one applies or applicants are of the wrong type.

- there is genuine scarcity: the skills sought are genuinely unavailable, meaning no end of pay increases will solve the problem.

The way to expose lack of pay competitiveness is to start by getting your recruiting methods right. Then you will find yourself in one of two situations:

- You get applicants but they are not interested in the pay you are offering. This means you have got a pay problem.

- You get no applicants at all. This means you've got a scarcity problem.

If, after following this approach, you deduce that pay is the problem then face up to it: it won't go away.

SUMMARY

Pay is a powerful persuader but treat it as a method of last (rather than first) resort.

LESSON TIME

THE 3 As

At this juncture we are going to introduce you to three principles. Simple though they are, the extent to which you adhere to these principles will determine how successful you are at recruiting skilled people.

Accessibility

This is the first principle. In your recruiting, the people you are targeting must be able to understand:

- what you are looking for (is it them?)
- what the job involves (is it what they want to do?)
- how much you are paying (are they going to be interested?).

The accessibility of advertisements is particularly critical and this is a subject we will be looking at in Chapter 8.

Availability

The people you are targeting must be able to get at you. You must be there, in the right place at the right time. Availability, funnily enough, is what most firms find hardest to get right.

Application

Being a successful skills recruiter means working at it. It can mean long and unsociable hours. You need to be aware of these demands and to make your plans accordingly. You also need to be aware that effort can sometimes be misdirected.

Collectively we call these three principles *The 3 As*. You can apply the 3 As to any difficult recruiting situation – not just skilled manual workers.

6

Understanding Skilled People

We are now going to turn to the kind of people we are trying to recruit. Skilled people – what do we know about them? Who are they and how do they behave? In particular we want to know what encourages skilled people to apply for jobs and what turns them off.

APPLYING FOR JOBS: HOW EMPLOYERS MAKE IT HARD FOR SKILLED PEOPLE

Chris is a highly skilled cnc machinist and he works for a company who produce prototypes and one offs mainly for the aerospace industry. The work is very interesting and Chris has been in the job for 4½ years. What has unsettled Chris is the possibility that his firm may be going onto shifts. This, the management say, is the only way they can expand.

Chris is paid £18 000 a year for his basic 39 hours. Overtime is plentiful so Chris's earnings in the last tax year came to about £25 000. Chris's aim is simple enough: he is looking for an interesting job where he can maintain these earnings without having to work shifts.

Glancing through the ads in the paper (which he does every week) Chris can always see plenty of opportunities for someone with his skills. In fact when he first started looking for another job he can remember thinking to himself he was going to be spoilt for choice. He decided initially to go for the big ads – the big displays advertising jobs for the most part in the big manufacturing companies. Usually

Continued on next page

these ads asked interested candidates to submit a CV. Chris had a CV already prepared so this presented no problem to him.

After three weeks of sending in CVs, Chris got his first interview – and his first difficulty. The interview was at 10am on a Thursday morning and it was to be followed by a psychometric test (Chris had no idea what this was). The timing of the interview gave Chris the problem of getting time off work. It was November and Chris had used up all of his floating holidays. Stumped for alternatives he rang the firm up to see if there was any chance of getting an interview on Saturday morning. The secretary he spoke to said she was sorry but this wasn't possible.

Chris ended up taking the day off. He got his wife to ring in to say he was sick. He didn't like doing this and he realised also that he would be losing a day's pay.

The bitter blow for Chris came when he was told at the interview that the pay for the job he was applying for was between £7 and £7.50 per hour. Chris explained about his current earnings and he and the interviewer agreed it was pointless carrying on.

Chris feels this experience taught him some lessons. He certainly isn't so quick to go for interviews any more.

Not many skilled people you come across are ever out of work. If they are, they tend to be out of work for short periods and that, when you think about it, is one of the benefits to having skills.

Not only are they likely to be in demand, skilled people are also likely to be the kind of people who work overtime on a fairly consistent basis. So the first point in putting together our little profile of the typical skilled person is that it is someone who is probably going to be at work between the hours of 8am and 6pm – or thereabouts. The exception may be Friday. (A point worth noting is that since the advent of the 39 hour week in the engineering sector it has become more and more customary for firms to finish early on Friday.)

Attending interviews during office hours is a problem for skilled people who are at work during the day. To compound the difficulty most people in the skilled category are still paid on the clock so losing time from work also means losing money – which is what happened to Chris. Like Chris too, most skilled people have chalked up a few bad experiences in their time. They have taken the time off, forfeited a day or half a day's pay and gone to the interview only to find out the wages are poor or the job has got hidden snags (or what they consider to be hidden snags).

This leads us onto the reasons why a lot of firms have conversion problems. Why is it, they ask us, we get loads of applicants then find the people we are interested in cancel their interviews – or don't turn up? The answer very often is simply this: the interviews are at times which clash with applicants' working hours.

OK, we can hear you saying, if these people have got such big problems attending interviews between 9 and 5 then why don't they ring in and say so? Why don't they tell us, for heaven's sake, and at least give us the option of fitting them in at other times?

Why don't they ring?

There are three possible explanations:

- They don't like to. They feel they're being awkward.

- They prejudge the outcome. Experience may have taught them that the answer to 'Can I come after 6 o'clock?' is bound to be no.

- If they find attending interviews difficult because they're at work during the day then the chances are they are going to find ringing you up in office hours just as difficult. Remember, most skilled people work in environments where making phone calls can be extremely difficult. Let's see what a couple of them have to say on this subject:

- *Tony:* 'We have to use the payphone in the works. It's noisy, then half the time the person you're trying to get hold of is in a meeting or the girl on the switchboard leaves you hanging on till your change runs out.'

- *Simon:* 'We can use the phone in the office for personal calls but the foreman can hear every word you're saying.'

What about people who work shifts? Surely they don't have these problems? Surely they have the benefit of free time during the day for getting to interviews?

Shiftworkers have their own problems. The shifts they work have all sorts of patterns. Some shifts are permanent shifts – for example there are people who work permanent nights or permanent 2pm to 10pm shifts. Some shifts, on the other hand, rotate so people's working hours change weekly or fortnightly or at other intervals. Some shiftworkers work Monday to Friday whereas others do shift patterns which take in the weekend. The permutations are almost endless.

With shiftworkers the difficulty for you (the recruiter) is knowing at the point of application:

- that you're in fact dealing with a shiftworker (people don't necessarily mention they're on shifts in their letters of application or on their CVs or in phone calls);

- what this means in terms of their day-by-day patterns of work, sleep and free time.

So unless you think to ask, you won't know whether the interviews you're inviting shiftworkers to attend are going to cause them problems or not. In a way, therefore, they are even harder to deal with.

MAKING IT EASIER FOR POTENTIAL JOB CANDIDATES

Tales from the Front Line

A factory manager we met a few years ago took the view that getting to the interview was a test of the candidate's interest in the job. 'If they're keen enough, they'll make sure they're there,' was the way he saw it. This was, as you have probably guessed, a factory manager who was suffering from particularly acute skills shortages.

Lesson: If you want to recruit skilled people be prepared to bend and make yourself *available*. In particular be prepared to do interviews out of normal hours. This means putting yourself out which is an example of where another of our 3 As, *application*, comes in. It also means you need to establish voice contact with applicants prior to setting up interviews. Speak to them and see what is a problem to them and what isn't.

Later in the book we will be looking at using telephone hotlines to recruit skilled people. Telephone hotlines (asking people to ring in between certain times) can be powerful recruiting tools providing they're set up in the correct way. Part and parcel of running a successful telephone hotline means taking heed again, of the availability principle. For example a telephone hotline which is only open between 9am and 5pm scores low on availability. The people who don't get home till 6.30pm won't be able to use it. And when you think about it, if the telephone hotline is the only way of applying for the job then the whole exercise can be completely counterproductive – in fact you can get less response than if you'd taken the simple route and asked for applicants to write in. There is a further availability lesson here – if you're trying to recruit skilled people give them more than one route of applying, eg a telephone hotline *and* the facility to apply in writing or send in a CV. Lots of choice like this enhances your availability even further and in consequence your ability to recruit.

PAY ACCESSIBILITY

Going back to our friend Chris for a moment, you will remember we left Chris spitting blood abut his bad interview experience and vowing to be more careful about applying for jobs in future. To Chris, being more careful means finding out what the rate of pay is *before* he goes to the interview.

Now this preconditioning by the applicant is OK if the rate of pay happens to be mentioned in the advertisement, but as we know this isn't always the case. Adverts frequently contain words like 'negotiable' and 'competitive'. Words like these can mean practically anything.

Suggesting to companies they put their rates of pay in advertisements is usually greeted by blank stares. Although more and more advertisements for skilled people do contain details of wages, there is still a reluctance on the part of many employers to go public on something which they view as essentially personal and confidential. Reasons given range from 'not company policy' to 'we don't want other firms in the area to know' and so on.

Chris, to give him his due, often rings up firms who put ads in the paper where there is no information on pay other than 'attractive' or 'commensurate with the responsibilities' or some other meaningless form of words. He does this when the job sounds interesting and bearing in mind his preconditioning he tries to find out the rate of pay. Frequently, though, the response he gets is that the company doesn't divulge rates of pay to telephone callers. Result? Chris gives the job a miss.

Not all skilled people are as persistent as Chris, however. Some simply don't bother to apply for jobs where the rate of pay isn't quoted. They take it as a sign that the pay's poor.

Information on your job (particularly the pay) needs to be *accessible* to skilled candidates. If you are reluctant to put your rates in your ads then you need to find another way of dealing with this problem. You will lose candidates otherwise. The next chapter has a few tips on how you can address this problem. Of course, one of the other great benefits of pay accessibility from your point of view is that you will automatically be filtering out candidates who are looking for more money than you can offer. In short, you won't be wasting your time interviewing the wrong people. In addition, it will stop you from starting to form the view you don't pay enough.

'APPLICANT-FRIENDLY' RECRUITMENT METHODS

Is there anything else about skilled people and the way they approach the job market which might be useful to recruiters?

Fifteen or so years ago we used to chastise employers who put 'send a CV' in their ads for skilled manual workers. 'Skilled people don't have CVs', we used to tell them, 'no wonder you don't get any applicants!'

Times change. These days a lot of skilled candidates *do* have CVs. They may even be in the majority. But equally there are a lot who don't and even more who don't bother to keep their CVs up to date so putting 'send a CV' in an ad and offering no other method of applying can still have an adverse effect on the number of replies you are going to get. The knack, as we have mentioned previously, is always to have more than one way of applying, such as 'send a CV or ring our special hotline between —— and ——'.

We need to mention here that two methods of application score particularly strongly in terms of attracting volumes of skilled applicants. These are:

• applications in person (open doors)

• phone-in applications (hotlines).

We will be returning to these preferred methods of application later in the book.

SUMMARY

Don't view skilled people as awkward or avaricious. Instead try to appreciate where they're coming from. Use recruiting methods which cater for the lives they lead and the concerns they have.

7

Sources of Skilled People

Where do you go to find skilled people? In this chapter we will look at sources of skilled people and see how they compare.

WORD OF MOUTH (NETWORKING)

Sourcing skilled people by putting the word round in the trade is a method normally associated with small firms operating in tightly-knit skills communities. Everyone knows one another. The network is ready made.

Larger firms have also been known to make use of networks. The familiar cash incentive to 'introduce' someone has helped many large firms to overcome skills shortages in the past.

Snags? The essence of networking is that it takes recruitment out of the hands of the company and, let's face it, it's hard to say no to someone's cousin or best mate – especially when there's a £100 incentive payment hanging on the outcome. Some firms stopped networking when families and extended families started to become a problem to them.

Verdict on networks: never a complete answer. Fails to provide choice. If you use networks use them in combination with other sourcing methods. In other words don't rely on them.

JOB CENTRES

Experiences vary enormously but the consensus view among recruiters we speak to is that Job Centres don't perform very well as sources of skilled people. The impression most have formed is that skilled people don't use Job Centres and because of this, there is a reluctance on the part of many employers to notify them of skilled vacancies.

Similarly, if you ask skilled people seeking work why they don't pay a visit to the Job Centre they will say 'There aren't any jobs in the Job Centre for people like us'.

But before we start going round in circles asking ourselves who is to blame for this situation let's consider a much more fundamental problem with Job Centres – their opening hours. When most skilled people are free to go job seeking (ie after work), Job Centres are shut. Thus, if we go back to our 3 As, Job Centres don't come out very well in terms of availability. The location of many Job Centres (in crowded town centre areas where parking is difficult) doesn't help either. One interesting and entirely anecdotal piece of information about Job Centres and skilled people is that the latter do make use of the former when they're out of work; when, in short, availability is of no longer a concern to them. For this reason alone simply dismissing Job Centres as sources of skilled people is a mistake.

Verdict on Job Centres: ignoring the fact that we all pay taxes to help fund them, Job Centres are free to the user and this is no bad thing (skilled recruitment is on the whole a world of expensive options). Use the Job Centre for your skilled vacancies but again, don't rely on them. Use them in combination with other sources.

RECRUITMENT CONSULTANTS (AGENCIES)

The big gripe most employers have about recruitment consultants is the fees they charge. In most cases consultants' terms of business flag up charges of between 15 and 18 per cent of annual pay for the kind of people we are talking about. In practice, though, it is usually possible to negotiate consultants down to 12 per cent or even less. One of the benefits to consultants is that most of them work on a no-placement/no-fee basis meaning it costs you nothing if the recruitment exercise fails.

How effective are recruitment consultants as sources of skilled people? Apart from the fees, the most frequently heard criticism of consultants is that they are high on promises and poor on delivery – reflecting, sadly perhaps, that a lot of so-called recruitment consultants are little more than telesales people, with no in-depth knowledge of what skilled jobs involve. They say 'yes' every time they get an enquiry simply because this is what they're trained to do. Unfortunately the end result (when they come up with no-one or a very poor selection) is that you feel your time has been wasted – the time you spent trying to explain the job and the time you spent listening to all the chat. Witness the number of firms who put 'no agencies' in their ads these days.

Looking at availability, some agencies have late nights and out of hours phone-in facilities which puts them a notch up on the average Job Centre. Others don't. Another factor to bear in mind is that at the end of the day an agency is only as good as its database (its files): a good agency will keep these up to date.

Verdict on agencies: watch out for the time wasters. In skilled employment the best agencies to use are the ones who specialise. These may be small agencies rather than the big names.

ADVERTISING

Putting an ad in the local evening paper is still probably one of the favoured methods of sourcing skilled people. Evening papers tend to have a 'job night' (Thursday seems to be favourite). Some also have special nights for particular kinds of job. On the whole it's best to stick to advertising on these job nights although some recruiters have expressed the concern that individual vacancies can get 'lost' in the sheer volume of recruitment advertising on that night. Our anecdotal evidence, however, suggests that a lot of skilled people only scan the ads on job night.

If you're looking for downsides with advertising in the local evening rag then one of the big ones is the price. The cost of big display ads can run into thousands of pounds, and advertising, of course, carries no guarantees. No-one suitable may apply and there's no way of getting your money back. As a matter of interest, in the course of our work we have come across a number of cases of companies who have run up five figure bills advertising for skilled people, with little or no result.

What about lineage ads? Rightly or wrongly, larger companies tend to shun lineage ads in *sits vac* (situations vacant) columns, feeling that such low-profile columns don't project a very good image; that size is what matters when it comes to catching the eyes of hard-to-find people. We will be looking at effective advertising in the next chapter but suffice to say at this point that what counts with recruitment ads for skilled people isn't size but accessibility and availability. Do remember this.

Tales from the Front Line

One of our candidates has got a rule-of-thumb with job ads. The bigger the ad, he reckons, the worse the pay.

Sits vac ads can be made to be very effective – as effective as big display ads, providing you pay heed to the 3 As. One good point about *sits vac* ads, apart from the price, is that they are conveniently broken down into sections such as 'technical', 'engineering', 'building' and so on. This means your ad doesn't get jumbled up with ads for care assistants and financial consultants, which is what happens with big displays.

What about other kinds of printed matter for recruiting skilled people?

Free sheets have made a big impact in recent years. Free sheets are usually quite cheap to advertise in, although they do have the disadvantage of being distributed in fairly tight geographical areas. You can of course overcome this problem by spending more and buying into series of free sheets where they are available. A lot of companies swear by free sheets and claim to have had good results. Our own experience is a little more mixed. We tend to use free sheets in addition to rather than in place of the local evening paper.

Newspaper groups in some areas put out dedicated recruitment journals. These tend to be weekly publications and contain listings of all the job ads plucked from their various titles. In other words your ad gets another showing free of charge, very often without you knowing and irrespective of whether you agree with it or not.

One kind of paper clearly to avoid for skilled recruiting is the local morning heavy which has a readership comprising mainly business and professional people.

Verdict on advertising: gets at most people hence very effective providing you use it properly (back to the 3 As). Read the next chapter which is all about getting the best results from advertising.

RECRUITING FROM OTHER AREAS

Companies in areas where skills shortages are rife have traditionally looked to casting their net a little wider, ie to where the skills they need may be in more plentiful supply. Areas associated with high unemployment are natural targets for this kind of activity. Companies have even been known to sometimes extend these searches overseas.

Verdict: We will be looking at recruiting in other areas in Chapter 11, Desperate Measures. For now, view this kind of activity as something loaded with potential difficulties and expense – and for those reasons, best avoided. If you can.

OPEN EVENTS

This is the company open day or open evening to which anyone can come along. The typical format for an open event is a guided tour followed by semi-formal chats about employment opportunities. Some firms really go to town with open events particularly with the kind of mass recruiting situations which go, for example, with the opening of new factories. Open events can and have been used with good effect for smaller recruiting exercises too – including filling a number of skilled vacancies. They have the drawback that anyone and everyone can come along but in our view this is a small price to pay for the opportunity of solving a serious skills shortage.

Our friends the 3 As come into play with open events and making them effective. How you advertise an open event is also critical.

Verdict: good providing you plan them properly. They give the facility for applications in person which is much favoured by the skilled person. The open event format is used for one of our preferred methods of recruiting in the next chapter.

OTHER SOURCES

We could go on and on with sources of skilled people. Some firms have used commercial radio to good effect; others have had hand bills printed and pushed through every letter box within a certain given radius of the factory. Doubtless as we write this book someone somewhere is sourcing skilled people off the Internet. It just goes to show that human inventiveness knows no bounds when it comes to solving a problem.

Verdict: if conventional sources won't work for you then the chances are you've got one of two problems:

Either: you lack 3 As. You're not tapping into your sources as effectively as you might and this is something you can put right. The next chapter deals with how you can make advertising work more effectively for you.

Or: the people you want are genuinely not there.

If these are your problems (either of them) then using other sources won't help you.

SUMMARY

Sources can be good or bad depending largely on how you use them. You can enhance the effectiveness of any source by applying the 3As. Don't see sources as alternatives to one another. Use multiple sources, not just one.

8

Using Advertising More Effectively

We have chosen advertising as the basis for our model method of sourcing skilled people for two reasons:

1. Everyone has used it; everyone is familiar with the way it works.

2. You have control over it from start to finish. You can apply the 3As and you're not relying, for example, on a recruitment consultant or someone down at the Job Centre to do it for you.

Advertising is expensive and skilled people are scarce. Sadly a lot of advertising for skilled people yields poor response and employers wonder why. In this chapter we will look at how to improve response to advertising and get better value for money.

ACCESSIBILITY AND ADVERTISING

With advertising, accessibility is the crunch issue. The people you are trying to recruit must be able to understand in one quick read that:

- the job is for them, someone with their skills;

- it's the kind of job they want to do (Type of work – does it involve shifts? Do you need them to travel? etc);

- it's paying the kind of wage they would be interested in;

- it's in an area they want to work in (something to remember when using lineage ads which may not contain your full address).

The one quick read test is important. Remember, your ad will be in the paper on job night along with dozens of others.

ACCESSIBLE JOB TITLES

Accessibility starts with job titles and the fact that job titles used by companies don't always reflect the common usage of words. For example, we had a company advertising recently for a manufacturing technician – a term which had a precise meaning to them but which could mean almost anything to anyone else. The job was in fact for a press toolsetter but any press toolsetter scanning the ads that night might be forgiven for not recognising that the job was for someone with their skills. Accessible job titles in ads are important because job titles are usually what sits in bold at the top of the ad and consequently what catches the reader's eye. People see a job title which strikes a chord with them and then they read the rest of the ad to see what it says. If no chord is struck then they read no further.

Lesson: when you put a job title in an ad don't automatically use the job title you use internally. Think about the kind of people you are trying to recruit and how they would view themselves (their trade). Use this terminology.

WHAT TO PUT IN RECRUITMENT ADVERTISEMENTS

Information about the Company

A lot of advertising copy is put together by advertising agents and in many ways we think this is a pity. They have a tendency to use up far too much of the available space with glowing descriptions of the firm, ie its PR image.

Skilled people won't be greatly impressed by the number of times the word 'excellence' can be squeezed into a 2 column, 10 centimetre ad but what *will* take their eye is information on how the job fits into the general scheme of things. For example, that a service engineer is a key figure in the firm's overall standing with its customers and so on. A lot of good skilled people seek self esteem ('I'm not just an irk with a box of spanners') and recognition of the important part they have to play strikes a happy chord with them.

Information about the Job

Skilled people are naturally interested in the kind of work they will be doing and the kind of equipment they will be using but this is precisely the kind of information professional copy writers omit or gloss over (in many cases out of ignorance). Acres of space will be devoted to what a wonderful team we all are but when it comes to the real nitty-gritty, what the job actually entails, we are often fed statements such as 'you will be carrying out maintenance duties in our modern factory'. Hardly a turn-on to anyone! If the firm is looking for a maintenance engineer then what might be far more pertinent information is a description of the machinery in the factory (anything interesting about it?) and, for example, what kind of fault finding is involved. This also helps candidates to decide whether the experience they have is relevant or not. Remember, they will be as concerned as you are about timewasting.

Information about the Conditions

Primarily this concerns things such as shifts, call-outs or any other mandatory arrangements in the job package. Make anything like this crystal clear. Incidentally, if a job is on days it is worth putting in 'no shifts' (which you might not think to do). In most skilled populations there are always some people trying to get away from shift work.

Information about the Pay

Here comes the crunch issue for many employers – putting the rate of pay in the ad and detailing bonuses, shift payments, expense allowances etc – in other words making your pay rates *accessible*.

The last thing we want to do is take issue with firms who are hesitant about putting details of pay rates in recruitment ads. We understand their hesitancy but we would like them at least to acknowledge two difficulties they are creating:

- *Some people won't apply*: notably people who have had the Chris type of experience mentioned earlier. Some people will even take the view that because it isn't advertised, the pay is poor.

- *You will get people applying who are beyond your reach*: looking for more money than you can offer. Unless you take some positive action to prevent it, the chances are this situation won't reveal itself until you get head to head in an interview. Then both parties will feel they have wasted their time.

When dealing with skilled people one practice we would strongly advise you to avoid is putting in your ads 'pay negotiable', 'attractive rates of pay' or any of the other standard phrases we have all used at some point in our careers.

How can we help firms who don't want to put their rates of pay in their ads?

The next subject we will be looking at is methods of applying – in what format you ask people to submit their application for the job and how you can enhance the response to the ad by methods which incorporate *availability*. One of the particular techniques we will be looking at is telephone hotlines – getting applicants to ring in on a special number and between specified times. Using telephone hotlines means that from the onset you have voice contact with the applicant and this gives you the opportunity you need to go into details of pay over the 'phone. So what you might include in your ad is something along the lines of ' . . . for more information on the job and the pay please ring us on (phone number) between —— and ——'.

METHODS OF APPLICATION (AVAILABILITY)

Methods of application and how you ask people to apply for the jobs you advertise are critical considerations. Most sourcing difficulties (too few or no applicants) are allied to methods of application which are inappropriate or which take little account of availability. With methods of application the usual choices are:

- write in
- send a CV

- ring us

- pop in and see us.

There are several minor variations on those themes, such as send us a fax (not, incidentally, advisable with skilled people because of the problem of getting access to a fax machine) or apply to the Job Centre (could be a new plant opening where the people to deal with applications aren't yet in place – take heed here of our earlier warnings about Job Centres and their out of hours availability).

Tales from the Front Line

The tailpiece to one ad for a skilled job we saw recently read, 'No phone calls or CVs. Consideration will only be given to applications received on an official application form. To apply for an application form, write to the personnel officer at the address given below. Previous applicants need not re-apply.'
Anyone interested?

We have commented already on:

- the decided preference among the skilled community for personal methods of application. 'Ring us' or 'pop in and see us' are by far the best way of getting good response to advertisements;

- the importance of having more than one method of application available to candidates thereby giving them choice.

For these reasons ads which offer 'pop in and see us' and/or 'ring us' are by far the most effective for sourcing skilled people.

Now we've got the best tools for the job. Let's see what we can do to sharpen them.

HOTLINES (PHONE-INS)

To enhance the performance of job hotlines we need to consider in more detail their *availability*. We have already looked at the difficulties skilled workers (other than shiftworkers) face when it comes to making telephone calls during normal office hours. For them this usually boils down to having to use pay phones or trying to make calls from work extensions with the ever-present fear of being overheard by the boss. Often these obstacles prove too much for people. The people who may be best for the job simply don't bother. But it is far easier for them if the facility to ring in is provided when they don't have these problems, ie when they get home from work. This is why job hotlines open early till late get by far the best results. Late, incidentally, means up to about 8.30 or 9pm.

Furthermore, past experience has shown that applying for a job is often an impulsive act and the impulse is strongest just after reading the advertisement. So a phone-in up to 8.30pm should be available on the night the ad appears. This will give the skilled people we want the chance to get home, have their meal, and a quick flick through the ads and still have time to make a call to you. It is even better if your hotline can be open on two consecutive evenings, ie the evening the ad appears and the following evening. This caters for those people who don't read the job ads straight away.

Always state in your ads *when* your hotline is open, eg 'you can call us on our special job hotline between 8am and 8.30pm today or tomorrow. One of our human resources advisers will be waiting to talk to you.' If you don't do this applicants will assume (incorrectly) that your hotline is open only during office hours. 'One of our human resources advisers will be waiting to talk to you' is a way of reassuring applicants that they won't be greeted by an answering machine or a grumpy security officer who has been left with the task of taking calls when the offices/factory is closed. Manning a job hotline calls for a bit of *nous* too – a task, therefore, that you should do yourself or share with a professional colleague. (Now you see where the *application* comes in – the third of our 3As.) The importance of being there, being the intelligent and informed voice on the end of the line, is revealed further in our next chapter where we will be looking at conversion – turning applicants into starters.

Why is it important to have your hotline on standby first thing in the morning? Don't forget shiftworkers and people who work unusual hours. You need to make your availability a feature for everyone.

A further feature of a really successful hotline is that it needs to be dedicated. By this we mean:

- not having it clogged up with other calls as, for example, the extensions in the human resources department will tend to be. People ringing from a pay phone will run out of change if they have to hold. People using the phone at work sur- rounded by flapping ears will hang up. Here a direct line facility commends itself enormously (see our chapter on resources – Chapter 10). Direct lines also circumvent the problem of switchboards closing at normal going-home times and putting calls onto works' night lines which might serve other (conflicting) purposes – such as the night shift's way of dialling out.

- reserving it for skilled applicants. Discouraging applicants for other jobs from using the same facility.

Tales from the front line

We had a case of a company with a new factory (greenfield site) and vacancies right across the board, including skilled. They invested about £3000 in a big ad in the local evening paper for a whole range of jobs. The ad offered applicants a hotline facility – a direct line into the human resources department open from 8am to 8pm. The mistake, of course, was that they gave this facility to everyone, including applicants for unskilled jobs such as assemblers and packers. The result? The hotline was jammed with calls from large numbers of unskilled applicants and only two skilled candidates succeeded in getting through. The company did much better when they advertised their skilled vacancies separately on another occasion.

Availability and running phone-in lines also involves careful diary management. Don't, for instance, fix up meetings on days when you are supposed to be manning the hotline.

Warning: firms offering phone-in facilities for respondents to ads frequently give the name of the person to ask for, eg 'ring Phil Smith on our special job line. . . .' They do this of course for perfectly laudable reasons – to introduce a personal touch into what otherwise may seem a very impersonal situation. From time to time (and partly for reasons of devilment) we try phoning up a few of these Phil Smiths to test out how good their availability really is. Often, alas, we hear 'Phil's not here – sorry' or 'Phil's been called into a meeting' or 'Can anyone else help you?' (Well, we don't know, do we?) Within the confines of carrying out a normal day-to-day management function achieving availability – bell-to-bell availability – can be tricky so don't try it.

There is a further point to not putting names in ads. Manning phone-ins is a chore, particularly out of hours, and you will find it far easier to cope with if you can share the duty turns with someone else.

OPEN SESSIONS

Open house, ie letting applicants pop in when they want to (no appointments) is another powerful method of sourcing applicants for skilled jobs.

Human resources managers tend to hold up their hands in horror when we suggest using open sessions. The idea of people strolling in off the street unsifted and unsorted seems like asking for trouble.

We will deal with handling open sessions in the next chapter and hopefully lay some of these fears to rest. Here we want to look at how to make open sessions successful from a sourcing point of view (getting the right people to call in and in reasonable numbers).

Here again *availability* is the key issue. Open sessions need to run on into the evening and this facility needs to be made clear in your advertisements: 'Call in and see us. We are open till 8.30pm this evening and tomorrow (Friday).' As with phone-in lines, two consecutive evenings pays dividends – the evening the ad appears and the evening after being favourite.

Here are a few more tips for running successful open sessions.

- Consider car parking. Don't put people off by having nowhere for them to park.

- Put plenty of signs up. Make it clear to people that (a) they're welcome, (b) where they've got to go (this is especially important 'after hours' when reception areas may be shut).

- Consider the 'sundown factor', especially on winter evenings. Dark or poorly lit entrances will put people off. Perhaps the works engineer could lay on some extra lighting for you?

- Again, on evenings when there is an 'r' in the month, check when the heating goes off. Make sure the rooms your open sessions are held in are warm.

- Have somewhere for people to sit in comfort. A coffee pot with a 'help yourself' sign on it is a nice little embellishment (the smell helps!). Put out some company literature for people to read if they have to wait.

- Do your one-to-ones somewhere out of earshot of people waiting their turn.

- *Most important*, as with phone-in lines, don't mix open sessions for skilled people with unskilled and other job candidates. Queues and crowds are major off-putters – especially to people whose time is valuable to them.

SUMMARY

Slapping an ad in the paper guarantees nothing except the bill. Make your ad work for you and source the market properly. If you want results put your effort into maximising *accessibility* and *availability*.

WORKSHOP

In this section of the book you have a chance to look at some advertisements for skilled people. See what you think about them and how you might improve them. To avoid giving offence the name of the company in each case is fictitious but each ad closely resembles an ad we have actually seen in print.

Our comments appear at the end of the section. Compare your conclusions with ours.

Barleygrow
Whole foods

We are part of the ZZ Foods group and due to rapid expansion of our Stubbleton site we now have vacancies for the following positions:

PRODUCTION CONTROLLER

GENERAL CLERK

MECHANICAL FITTER
Working Shifts

SALES OFFICE ASSISTANT

Apply in the first instance to:

Job Centre
River Street
Stubbleton on Wye
Herefordshire
ST99 9XX

We are an equal opportunities employer.

ENGINEERING VACANCIES

ELECTRICIANS AND FITTERS

Blowcast Mouldings is one of the UK's foremost producers of quality precision die-castings for the automotive and aerospace industries. We urgently require experienced electrical and mechanical engineers for our maintenance team.

Electricians work a four crew continuous system entailing the working of 4 × 12 hour shifts followed by four rest days.

Electrical applicants need fault finding skills on modern die-casting machines and machine tools.

Fitters are employed on a four day rota and need to have mechanical maintenance skills including hydraulics and pneumatics.

Please write with full details to:

Michelle Tighe
Personnel Officer
Blowcast Mouldings Limited
P O Box 10
Sloeborough
Hants
SB99 9XX

FASTLANE – COMPETING TO WIN

Skilled Fitter

An experienced Fitter is required to work in our vehicle maintenance department.

The ideal applicant will be conversant with mixed fleet requirements ranging from light vans to HGVs. A clean HGV licence is essential.

Average earnings for 39 hours are £270.

Interested? Application forms are available from:

Personnel Department
Fastlane Logistics UK Limited
Stoke Midlington
Berks
SM12 1AA

Telephone: 0123 456 789 (extension 999)

An invitation from

 OGGYDINS

to meet us on

EITHER

Saturday 30 November at 10.00am

OR

Wednesday 4 December at 7.30pm at our Main Gate in Asquith Street, North Noddington

Substantial investment in production facilities has ensured our leading place in the pet foods market. To meet this challenge we need to recruit enthusiastic people to help us implement our dynamic plans for further development. Opportunities exist in most categories ranging from packers, fork lift truck drivers to fully skilled maintenance engineers.

If you have the relevant experience then you should come along.

Alternatively if you can't make it, write in or phone Alison Smith on 0111 123 456 (direct line)

RSVP

BENCH HAND £8 p/h + o/t. City Centre. Contract Toolroom. Press tools. Jigs. Fixtures. Phone Alan on 0123 456 789. Tonight or tomorrow up to 7.00pm. Altools.

 **owercutter**

SERVICE ENGINEER
North West
£22k + Car

Powercutter UK is a wholly owned subsidiary of the Powercutter Corporation which is among the top five machine tool companies worldwide.

As part of the planned expansion of our UK field service team we are seeking an additional Service Engineer to cover the North West of England. Following an intensive course of product training at our parent company's factory in Baltimore USA the successful candidate will be responsible for all customer service calls on the territory.

An electrical background in the machine tool industry is essential which must include cnc machining centres and lathes. A knowledge of Fanuc control systems is also desirable. Applicants must be resident in the North West (Greater Manchester preferred).

Informal interviews for this position will be held at the Windyridge Hotel, Windyridge Road, Warrington, on Thursday 3 October 1996. Please phone Mike Dennis on 0123 999 999 (lines open till 9 pm tonight and tomorrow) to make an appointment.

Powercutter UK Limited
Unit 9
Stones Bridge Industrial Estate
Stones Bridge
Bedfordshire
SB1 1AA

WHAT WE THINK . .

Barleygrow Wholefoods

Here we have one skilled job (a mechanical fitter), mixed in with a number of others (more on this point in a moment). Accessibility is plainly very poor to the point of being non-existent. We imagine the job is to do with maintenance but this isn't made clear anywhere. The shift patterns applicants will be expected to work are likewise not detailed and there is no mention of pay whatsoever – not even a perfunctory 'good' or 'competitive'. Methods of application are restricted to just one (the Job Centre) and even then it isn't clear whether applicants are supposed to write or call in.

Barleygrow, we feel, would benefit enormously in response terms if they could provide more nitty-gritty information about the job. For example, if it is a maintenance position, some information about the kind of plant would be useful together with what kind of qualifications and experience applicants should have. All this would enable applicants to decide whether the job is for them or not. The shift patterns are also essential information from the applicant's point of view ('is this a job I want to do') and there needs to be some indication of pay or the facility to discuss pay pre-application.

Response would also be enhanced if Barleygrow could offer two or three different ways of applying. A phone-in facility or an open session or both should be included, in our view, to give maximum availability. If the Job Centre is retained as one of the options then it should be explained to applicants whether they need to call or write. If it is the former then the Job Centre's opening hours should be listed. Powerful sourcing methods such as phone-ins and open sessions should be restricted to skilled applicants only, hence the mechanical fitter needs to be advertised separately. If not, there is the very real possibility that the company will be swamped with applicants for the other jobs. The phone-in line will be jammed, the reception area will be chock-a-block with people for the open session, and the skilled applicants will be put off.

Blowcast Mouldings

The plurals (electricians and fitters) indicate this company has several vacancies. These jobs are on shifts. The electricians appear to work a four on/four off continental pattern and, from the 'continuous system', we assume this alternates between days and nights (although this isn't made clear). What is meant by the four day rota for fitters is a bit of mystery although again it would seem to indicate a four on/four off pattern. In other words, the company's attempt to explain its shifts has largely got lost in the phraseology. They know what they mean but does anyone else?

The fact that the jobs are in maintenance is explained in the small print but not in the heading. What applicants will be working on is made reasonably clear (ie die-casting machines and machine tools) so they will be able to judge to some extent whether they are suitable or not. Pay isn't mentioned at all. Again we have only one way of applying which is to write in to the personnel officer.

We think the response to this ad can be enhanced by getting the word *maintenance* into the job titles at the top (eg maintenance electrician and maintenance fitter). This would help satisfy the 'one quick read' accessibility test.

Advertising the jobs separately would be preferable also, but as both are skilled it doesn't raise the same kind of problems that Barleygrow would have with their mix of skilled and others.

The description of the shift pattern could be much better and we would have thought that the terminology four on/four off continental shifts could safely be used since applicants for this kind of position would know what it means.

As with Barleygrow there needs to be information on pay or the facility to discuss pay pre-application.

Whether plurals help in job titles is a matter for conjecture. Some practitioners think they enhance response (more jobs, more chance of success) whereas others (us included) think they present a picture of an organisation which is straining and cracking as a result of staff turnover.

Like Barleygrow, Blowcast Mouldings could also get some spin off from offering prospective candidates two or three different ways of applying including phone-ins, open sessions or both.

Fastlane

This is an advertisement for a vehicle mechanic, which isn't apparent until you read the small print. Accessibility is otherwise reasonable with the pay clearly stated. We assume this company with its mixed fleet is going to need someone with a Class I HGV licence but this isn't made clear. Again, the applicants will be left wondering whether they are suitable or not.

It is not clear whether interested parties should write or phone in for the application form. From the address in full and the phone number at the foot the inference is that either is acceptable. The phone in facility gives no indication of times so whether the intention was to add availability or not is impossible to say. Fastlane's personnel department clearly feel they need to have sight of an application form before they commit themselves any further so it seems a fairly safe bet we will be in for a long drawn out selection procedure here.

With this ad, enhancement of response could best be achieved by:

- advertising for an HGV mechanic (in big, bold letters at the top). This is a case of where an internal job title (skilled fitter) has a multiplicity of meanings to the outside market – most of them unconnected with vehicles;

- opening up the methods of application to include phone-ins, open sessions or both.

If phone-ins are used then:

- from/to times need to be inserted;

- a direct line would be better than an extension off a switchboard.

Doggydins

This is a novel and eye-catching way of presenting recruitment advertising which deserves a pat on the back just for that. There is also a very creditable attempt to drive in some availability with two open sessions plus the facility to write in or phone in on a direct line. With the phone-in, however, no times or days are given and callers are invited to ask for a name (Alison

Smith), which begs the question: What happens if she's not there?

The main let down with the ad is on the accessibility front. Maintenance engineers (the only skilled category) will have to plough through the whole ad before they find out whether or not there are jobs for them in Doggydins's big expansion plans. What these jobs involve and whether they're on shifts is left to the imagination. Perhaps the nature of the industry may offer some clues. Pay apparently does not merit a mention. Again there is the problem of mixing skilled with other vacancies, including unskilled.

How could we improve on this one?

Why not 'An invitation to maintenance engineers . . .' set at the top with some detail on the job and requirements for applicants written into the text at the expense, perhaps, of some of the bally-hoo about the company's dynamic plans. The other jobs need to be left out because of the problem of using powerful sourcing techniques for categories of workers in abundant supply. We need some reference to pay, too – as with Blowcast and Barleygrow.

What about the plurals (maintenance engineers)? Here it is clear that the vacancies have arisen because of expansion so the feeling of joining a sinking ship doesn't present itself.

As we have said, there has been a very honest attempt at availability which could be enhanced by:

- stating start times and days for phone-ins inclusive of any after-hours facility;

- not restricting callers to one person.

Altools

This, when you look at it, isn't a bad little *sits vac* ad which, providing it appears in the right classified section on the right night, will probably do quite well.

In terms of accessibility the ad tells us precisely what the job is, what the work entails and the rates of pay. Any bench hand toolmakers glancing through the ads will spot this one and see practically all they need to know pre-applying – even the location (city centre).

'Phoning Alan' may not be such a good idea because if Alan is the boss it's a safe bet he won't be standing by the phone all day and halfway through the night. Seven o'clock in the evening may be a bit early to end a phone-in so Alan could probably gain by sticking round for another hour or two (or investing in Star Services and diverting the calls to his home phone).

There is only one method given to apply but it is a powerful one and, taken within the constraints of a cheap small ad, the sourcing potential is good.

Powercutter

This is a company recruiting out of area for a job which is out of area too – in this case a field based service engineer. The accessibility of the ad is quite good although perhaps the inclusion of 'machine tools' somewhere in the heading might have helped. The information includes the pay and type of vehicle.

The company have adopted a slightly different approach to availability. They have set up local interviews at a hotel though there is no indication that out of hours interviews are available. They have set up a phone-in line open till 9pm on two consecutive nights for applicants to make appointments. The inference is that there will be no vetting at this stage or sifting out of unsuitable applicants. Callers will automatically get an interview – and perhaps this is intentional, ie the company may feel it is going to enhance response if applicants know they're definitely going to get the opportunity to meet the company face to face. There is only one method of applying which is a weakness. For instance, a candidate who is away on holiday or has some other problem on 3 October may feel there is no point in making contact.

A further weakness is that an individual is named in the ad (Mike Dennis) which begs the question, what happens if Mike Dennis isn't there? We don't know if the telephone number in the ad is Mike Dennis's direct line or whether the calls will be routed through a switchboard.

Improvements? We think some indication that after-hours interviews are available on 3 October will help. Other methods of application will also help. To avoid the 'Mr Dennis isn't here, sorry' problem it might be better to invite callers to 'ring us' or 'ring one of our human resources staff' or some such phrase.

9

Converting Applicants into Starters

Sourcing skilled people is only half the story. The next problem is *conversion* – getting the people who apply onto the payroll. More than three-quarters of the firms we talk to have conversion problems.

> Rumbletum Snackfoods operate a state-of-the-art food processing and packaging plant in the heart of a large industrial area. Their recruitment problem is maintenance technicians. The key skills here are fault finding, rectifying and carrying out preventative maintenance on a range of high speed machines, some of which have sophisticated computerised controls.
>
> The people Rumbletum are seeking need primarily to have electrical core skills and Rumbletum have twigged already the need to make this clear (accessible) in their ads. In fact, Rumbletum don't seem to have any difficulty in attracting people. Using phone-in lines and 8 to 8 open sessions they get, on average, over 20 enquiries per ad. What's disappointing though is the conversion rate of applicants to starters. Approximately 50 per cent of the people they invite for interviews don't turn up. Fifty per cent of the people they offer jobs to decline or fail to start.
>
> Rumbletum's human resources director is lost for answers. Are they doing something wrong? If so, what? Are they selecting the wrong people? Or is it that people can't be relied on these days?

Rumbletum's experiences illustrate how candidate fall out can occur at two stages: pre-interview and post interview/pre-employment. Let's look at both.

CANDIDATE FALL OUT

Pre-interview Fall Out

Properly organised early to late phone-ins and open house sessions have tremendous potential as *sourcers*. They bring in the numbers – bearing in mind that numbers means numbers relative to people with scarce skills. So, providing you don't mix skilled with other vacancies you are not likely to be inundated with telephone callers or people strolling in off the street (this being a major concern to a lot of the practitioners we talk to). If there is a likelihood it is that you will be twiddling your thumbs for large chunks of the time.

Nevertheless in these free for alls there is still a need for you to keep your conversations brief. With phone-ins for instance, you don't want the line blocked for half an hour while you deal with one caller. The same applies to open houses where you need to avoid queues building up.

The ground you need to cover is as follows:

- *More information about the job*: Expand on what's in the paper but explain that this isn't an interview.

- *Pay*: What's the applicant looking for? Discussing pay is especially important if you happen to be one of those firms who don't like putting their rates in ads.

- *Snags*: Is there anything about the job which might make it unpleasant or anti-social in some people's eyes? If so, mention it and see what reaction you get.

- *Broad suitability*: Is the person you're talking to a time-waster or in the broadest terms can he/she be considered for the job? This is a simple yes or no.

If you're still seeing eye to eye with the applicant after this then move on without more ado to fixing up an interview. Say, for instance, 'We'd like to get you back when we can spend a bit more time with you. How are you fixed over the next few days?'

More diary management now: after those phone-ins and open houses you will need to have time set aside for carrying out interviews. You will need to do this quickly (next few days *means* next few days) and you need to set aside out of hours times too (availability). We have seen already how a lot of pre-interview fall out is due to lack of availability. If you've followed the approach so far this shouldn't happen.

So where did Rumbletum go wrong?

The answer is they lost the momentum. Instead of moving on swiftly from sourcing to interviewing they got themselves bogged down in a lengthy and ponderous selection procedure.

First, Rumbletum gave the applicants they sourced one of their standard application forms to take away and fill in. Telephone callers received their application forms through the post. Instructions were given to send the forms back straight away but no mention of interviews was made at this stage. Why not? Because Rumbletum's HR team felt they needed to see an application form *before* they committed themselves and a line manager to a full-blown interview. The risk, they felt, was that they might be wasting their time with some applicants.

OK, not unreasonable you may say, but if a week is a long time in politics then take it from us it's an eternity in scarce skills recruitment. By the time Rumbletum got their forms back a fortnight had passed. By the time they got round to phoning people up and asking them to come in for interview they were well into week three. What happened with their interviews? Some people declined to come; some accepted then later cancelled; some simply didn't turn up. Some may have already found another job.

Perhaps it's obvious that the longer it takes to process applications the greater the chances of incurring fallout. Sometimes, however, it's necessary to state the obvious.

Post interview/pre-employment Fall Out

Let's stay with Rumbletum and their experience for the moment. You will recall that 50 per cent of the people Rumbletum offered jobs to didn't start for one reason or another.

Rumbletum's selection process consisted of two interviews – a preliminary and a shortlist. The numbers on the shortlist depended on the number of vacancies they had. The preliminary interview included a selection test.

Counting the weeks off from their original sourcing exercise (phone-in or open house), the preliminary interviews took place in weeks 4, 5 and 6; the second interviews went into weeks 7 and 8. On average, therefore, it was taking around two and a half months to get candidates from where they first expressed interest in the job to where they got an offer of employment. This is of course far too long and asking for trouble. But before you start sneering just check how long *your* company's selection procedures take. You could be in for a shock.

Asking Rumbletum's HR team why they couldn't speed things up a bit put them on the defensive. Two objections came up:

- They didn't want to do anything which might impair the integrity of their selection process. Taking shortcuts, as they put it, might reduce fall out but what did they gain if the result was poor selection? Surely this was the route to incurring even higher labour turnover?

- They had other vacancies to deal with, apart from just maintenance technicians. Prioritising one group could only be done at the expense of another.

SELECTION PROCEDURES

As with Rumbletum, HR practitioners tend to get very uptight if you suggest their selection procedures are long-winded.

Application, the third of our 3 As, isn't just about putting in the hours. It is also to do with being able to dedicate yourself to the task of filling skilled vacancies and, as a consequence, being able to reduce the length of time you spend on selection procedures. This is not as easy as it seems. The world doesn't stop for skilled recruitment. All the thousand and one problems you normally have to deal with will still be there.

Chapter 10 (Resources) suggests ways of taking the pain out of recruiting skilled people but some pain is bound to remain. However, perhaps the best way to view this is that if you do recruitment our way it should be relatively short lived. Rumbletum, because of the fall out problems they were having, found themselves back in recruiting situations time and time again; the pain went on and on.

Now let's turn to what you can do to speed up your selection procedures and cut down candidate fall out.

- *Single out your skilled vacancies*: These and only these will be the ones to which you will be giving the accelerated treatment. In effect you will be prioritising them.

- *Vet applications at the sourcing stage* (over the phone or face to face if it's an open session): Fix up interviews with those who pass the broad suitability test. Ideally do your interviews within three working days.

- *Application forms*: By all means use application forms. Give these to the candidates you propose to interview and ask them to bring the completed form to the interview. Don't waste time sending them backwards and forwards in the post.

- *Interviews*: Try to do your selection in one interview or, if you need two interviews (one with HR and one with line management), do them end on (one after the other).

- *Confirm interview appointments in writing (by letter)*: You will find this gives you a better turn-up rate. People habitually respond better to anything in writing.

- *Selection tests*: A lot of tests do little to enhance the selection process. Take a harsh look at selection tests *vis à vis* skilled people. If in doubt cut them out.

- *Job offers*: Move on quickly to offering jobs. Phone successful candidates first – or ask them to pop in. Go through the job offer verbally with them. Clear up any areas of doubt. Get commitment on a starting date (when can you hand your notice in?) Confirm the offer in writing the same day.

By compressing selection procedures in this way it will automatically reduce fall out and step up your conversion rate. One advantage to making job offers verbally is that if the candidate declines or bombards you with misgivings then you can move onto the second choice candidate straight away. Frequently candidates don't bother to tell you if your job offer doesn't suit them for some reason (or if they've been bought off). More often than not you end up chasing them to find out what's going on when they don't turn up on the first morning. Then of course you've lost several days, meaning the trail may have gone cold with second choice candidates.

Tales from the Front Line

The longest selection procedure we have on record for a skilled manual job is six months. This was a large company whose selection procedures involved four separate interviews with different managers interspersed with long silences. Amazingly the gentleman concerned stuck the course and ended up joining the company – a tribute, surely, to his staying power!

Two final points on selection procedures:

1. (Rumbletum's concern) Yes, you could well end up with people on the interview list who would not otherwise have got there, ie your quick vettings failed. This is a snag but in our view is a small price to pay for solving skills shortages. On the whole, we find experienced interviewers are not often wrong in their snap judgements.

2. You will still get some fall out. There will still be people applying whose intentions aren't serious or who get bought off or who are just plain unsatisfactory.

WHAT IS SUCCESS?

Success is always relative to the task. In this case the task is recruiting skilled people who are scarce. In some categories they are very scarce indeed. Success, therefore, both in sourcing and conversion terms will usually be measured in ones and twos rather than dozens. You need perhaps to reflect on this before you dismiss, for instance, your phone-in session which yielded just a handful of calls as a total flop. The agony for scarce skills recruiters can consist of sitting in the office long after everyone else has gone waiting for the phone to ring and finding it doesn't ring very often. Read what we've got to say in the next chapter about direct telephone lines and using the call diversion facility which comes with BT Star Services. This will enable you to take your calls at home.

SUMMARY

When it comes to selection treat hard-to-find skills categories differently. Be flexible. Give these people priority and put them on a fast track. In this way you will keep candidate fall out to a minimum. More of the people you select will start.

10

Resources

We have said a lot in this book about application: putting in the hours and dedicating specific time to skills recruiting. Yet we appreciate that we are directing these messages at people who already see themselves as stretched to the limit – people like you.

In most medium- to large-sized firms the burden of work associated with skills recruiting will fall on the HR departments and these, as we know, have suffered more than most in the slimming-downs and delayerings of recent years. Some firms (not all of them small) don't have dedicated HR staff. Here the extra work will fall on line managers who are going to find it even harder to give skills recruitment the input it requires.

In this chapter we want to look at ways of making skills recruitment more palatable. In doing this we must bear in mind the financial constraints under which most firms operate these days. It would, for example, be very nice to have an additional member of staff to deal exclusively with skills recruiting but for most firms this would be entirely out of the question.

ORGANISATION

Being organised will help make skills recruiting easier for you.

We have already looked at diary management – avoiding commitments on days when you are running open sessions or hotlines and giving yourself time slots for interviews in the period immediately following sourcing exercises such as these. If you are in HR, being organised extends to organising line managers too – making sure, for example, line managers are going to be there (available) when you plan to get the candidates in for interview. Making sure you won't have to ask the candidates to come back on another occasion therefore increasing the risk of fall out.

A good tip is to have some information packs pre-prepared for your phone-in and open sessions. These needn't be anything fancy. An A4 envelope will do containing, for example:

- an invite to interview letter with blank spaces for the candidate's name and the time and date of the interview;

- job description (simple);

- application form.

You can hand out these packs to people who pass your broad suitability test. With telephone callers you can send your packs off by first class post.

For phone-in sessions, equip yourself with several A4 sheets of sticky labels. When you take callers' names and addresses write them straight onto the labels. You can then stick your label right onto an A4 envelope containing one of your information packs. Take photocopies of your sheets of labels which will give you a permanent record of your callers.

Being organised is also a learning process. As you do more and more sourcing exercises you will find ways (your own ways) of ironing out the wrinkles.

STAFF

Availability is much easier if you can share it with someone – bearing in mind the someone needs to be competent to talk about the job and its requirements and competent to judge the caller's suitability for an interview or not. Sharing the unsocial hours is a particular help. Two or more people sharing the duty turns with phone-ins and open sessions was the reason why we advised earlier against putting individuals' names in ads.

The extent to which you are involved in skilled recruiting will determine whether or not you need to consider making more permanent arrangements for these out of hours activities. For instance, if you are only doing two or three skilled recruiting exercises a year then you will probably be happy to grin and bear it. If, on the other hand, you are a big firm with a more or less ongoing requirement then it might be worth looking at the pros and cons of putting HR staff on shifts. Please don't dismiss this suggestion out of hand. Viewed as an alternative to long hours shifts may be more acceptable than you think.

REWARDING EFFORT

No-one has yet made their big career break by being good at recruiting skilled people. It is, sadly, yet another of those no glory jobs.

Nitty-gritty human resources practitioners and line managers in production and engineering – the people who will be doing the hard graft associated with skills recruiting – are not the kinds of people who fall into the 'fat cat' league; far from it. They are, in many cases, people who are paid quite modest salaries. Often they are salaried staff who are not paid for any extra hours they do – and, because they're busy people involved in day-to-day issues, taking time off in lieu is not a practical reality for them either.

In a lot of hard graft industrial situations recognition for a good job well done can, as we all know, be singularly lacking. Recognition in its simplest form is a 'thank you' – preferably from someone at the top. Yet how many HR practitioners do we come across who have put in the hours on skills recruiting, often completely unsupported, who have received not one word of appreciation for it?

To give skills recruiting the buzz it needs there has to be some feelgood to it. Given the restraints on having financial incentives for skills recruiters then somewhere along the line the hard work has got to be recognised somehow. Full marks, therefore, to the Chief Executive who took a personal hand in organising an open evening and laid on a very nice buffet for the staff afterwards. This may sound trivial but staff have to feel motivated about doing skills recruiting or it won't work.

PHONES

For sourcing purposes you will need to set up dedicated tele-phone hotlines from time to time.

The answer here is simple – if you haven't already got one, install a direct line into your office and have a rule that no-one uses it on phone-in days. If you're a big operation you may need more than one direct line.

BT offer a facility called Star Services – the advent of which has made life for skills recruiters a whole lot easier. With Star Services you can, for a very reasonable price:

• divert your calls to any number you like;

• divert your calls on busy – again to any number you like.

We mentioned in the last chapter that one of the difficulties with sourcing skilled people is that there are never going to be enough of them. Success in recruiting needs to be measured in terms of the scarcity. Depending on the scarcity of the skill, calls on phone-in lines can be few and far between.

The great advantage of a Star Services facility is that you don't have to stay in the office on phone-in nights. You can divert the calls onto your home number. In the past, recruiters who have recognised the need for availability have been known to put their home phone numbers in ads so evening callers can get through. With a Star Services call diversion you don't have to do this. The number appearing in the ad will be the office direct line. This will avoid the problem of getting nuisance calls at home.

Two points to bear in mind if you use Star Services and divert your hotline on to your home number:

• Consider your office to home journey. How long does it take? What's going to happen to the calls when you are on your journey? One answer to this problem is to get someone in the family (suitably schooled) to field the calls for you – taking names and numbers and promising you'll call back shortly is the best way. If this isn't feasible let a colleague take the calls while you journey home then transfer the line when you ring in to say you've landed.

• Don't forget to undivert the line when you get into the office the next morning. This is especially important where you are doing two-day phone-ins, otherwise you will be left wondering why you are not getting calls on your second day. The phone will be ringing at home instead.

The 'divert on busy' facility with Star Services is useful to skills recruiters because it enables you to handle more than one incoming call at a time. You can divert your hotline on busy onto another direct line or onto your main switchboard. If you do the latter you must give your switchboard some warning of what might happen and instructions on what to say, for example:

- take the caller's name and number;

- is the caller at home? In which case say someone will get back to them straight away;

- if they're at work, get their home telephone number, together with some idea of when they will be back. Assure them that they will get a call;

- if they're not on the phone get a number on which they can be contacted.

Warning: If a hotline is continuously engaged, particularly if the caller has tried several times, a natural thing to do is to try dialling in on the firm's directory number.

In this case two situations need to be avoided:

1. Switchboard operators who are confused by what the caller is saying ('I'm ringing your other number and it's engaged all the time').

2. Switchboard operators telling callers 'sorry it's nothing to do with us'.

Briefing switchboard operators may be a good idea anyway, irrespective of whether they are directly involved or not.

FUNDING

A lot of skills recruiting is underfunded and nowhere is this felt more than with advertising.

Take as an example a precision engineering business we visited some time ago which, according to its managing director, was turning away £250 000 a year in sales because of skills shortages. Yet this same managing director refused point blank to sanction advertising in the local evening rag which would have cost him all of £400. Asked why, he said he felt £400 was too much.

This particular managing director may be an isolated case but what is more frequently encountered is the kind of company who have tried advertising and given up because it didn't work (such as Gripnuts in Chapter 5). Nine times out of ten, of course, the advertising concerned lacked the accessibility and availability factors it needed to give it clout. But once the view that advertising wasn't a lot of use had been formed, it got the embargo treatment from then on.

Getting adequate funding for skills advertising is a challenge to your powers of persuasion, though we would hope that even the most obdurate top management could be talked into giving 'something different' a try.

Of course, advertising *does* cost a lot, though one suggestion, if the budget is tight, is to try a small ad in the sits vac columns with just a phone-in facility.

For example:

MULTI SPINDLE SETTER £16k + o/t. No shifts. Leading turned parts company. Good prospects. Phone Whizzrounds on 0123–456789 for details (direct line) up to 9pm tonight/tomorrow.

Not ideal, but what this ad does have is accessibility and availability. Potential applicants know what the job is and what it pays. It's also made easy for them to apply.

One drawback to our sits vac ad you will have spotted is that it restricts methods of applying to phoning in. This is because inviting candidates to call or write in would have necessitated putting in the firm's address and potentially doubling the cost of the ad.

Perhaps the main point here is to remind you that a good ad doesn't have to be a big ad. Its accessibility and the extent to which its methods of applying satisfy the availability test is all that really counts.

USING RESOURCES EFFECTIVELY

Application can be misdirected and it is not uncommon to come across firms who expend vast amounts of time and effort on recruitment exercises which yield nothing or next to nothing. The reason is usually that they are using methods which are wrong – or methods which are right but incorrectly applied.

To illustrate the latter let's return to the example of the HR department in the new factory, who spent large sums on advertising and a grand open evening but made the mistake of mixing their skilled with their other vacancies. These people worked very hard but all they got for their application was a lot of candidates for unskilled jobs – people who could have been sourced in far less painful ways. Furthermore, as the factory manager reminded them afterwards, it was the skilled people who needed to be on board first. Result: largely wasted effort, poor use of resources (cost of ad) and the prospect of having to do the exercise all over again on a skilled jobs only basis (more effort and resources).

Because skills recruiting is so demanding in terms of resources it is important (always) to ensure you are getting the right results – bearing in mind that success in scarce skills recruiting has a different meaning to success in other fields.

The capital sin is to compound failure with further failure and we wince every time we see companies advertising time and time again using precisely the same formula, except that the ads have a habit of getting bigger and more flowery and the inevitable warnings to previous applicants not to write in again creep in. This is precisely how firms succeed in running up five figure advertising bills, still with little success.

Apart from the cost factor, repeating advertising on a regular basis needs to be viewed critically for the following reasons:

- You are hitting the same readership with essentially the same message and you will find yourself a victim of the law of diminishing returns. With each ad you will, as a general rule, get a progressively poorer response.

- Applicants are put off by firms they see advertising a lot. 'What's wrong with the place?' they say to themselves. 'Why can't they keep people?' In extreme cases firms develop bad reputations for always having vacancies. In short, repetitive advertising can soon become counterproductive.

If your advertising satisfies the accessibility and availability criteria and if the response you are getting is still poor then you need first of all to run through the following checklist (ie *before* you contemplate re-running the ad).

- Is the media right? Are you using the newspaper which skilled people in your area read? In most cases this will be the local evening rag.

- Did your ad go in on job night?

- Did you see the ad? Did the newspaper print it properly? Whole paragraphs left out of ads (rendering them nonsensical) is not unknown. What is far more common is a wrong digit in the phone-in number. This is worth checking out too. Most newspapers incidentally are quick to own up to their errors and will offer to re-run the ad at no further charge. It is worth mentioning though that you will have less comeback on the paper if the ad has been dictated verbally. Faxed copy is preferable so that there can be no dispute about what you asked for.

- Did you notice where the ad actually appeared in the newspaper? We had an instance where a display ad we placed for a client turned up several pages removed from the main body of recruitment advertising (next to the crossword puzzle!) Complain like fury if this happens. Demand a free insert.

- Did you advertise in a 'funny week'? These include weeks preceding and during main holiday periods.

Tales from the front line

Those of you who use advertising agents will know how they sometimes produce artwork (logo, border styles etc) for your approval prior to the actual copy for the ad being agreed. Apart from the header (the job title) and the bit at the bottom about how to apply they fill up the rest of the space with a kind of gobbledygook which resembles Latin. One of our clients told us the tale of how an ad of theirs actually appeared in this form. The agency concerned immediately offered to foot the bill and apologised profusely for their mistake. The surprise for the firm, though, was the response they got to this ad which was excellent. The ad incidentally offered a phone-in facility and an open evening – proof indeed that these methods work!

No response at all to an ad should invite immediate suspicion:

- Check for faults on phone-in lines. We had a sobering case where a firm ran a phone-in line on two consecutive days.

The line had Star Services facilities and the human resources officer decided on the first evening to take the calls at home. Accordingly she diverted the office direct line to her home number as she left, getting her spouse to field the calls while she was on her journey. On the whole she had a very good evening with eight promising enquiries for two vacancies which had previously proved quite hard to fill. Day two of the phone-ins was, however, singularly disappointing. The phone didn't ring all day. Unfortunately for the human resources officer, she didn't discover until it was too late that she had forgotten to undivert the phone. The phone could have been ringing all day but in an empty house!

• With open evenings check for obvious bogeys, eg the sign directing applicants fell down or got taken away by some well meaning janitor (it's happened!). Temporary security staff have also been known to completely wreck open evenings ('Crikey, I'm sorry, I've been telling people you went home hours ago').

Once you've exhausted these checklists it is time to take stock. What message is the market giving you? Is there no-one out there? Are you paying enough? And, rather than invest more money in repetitive advertising, perhaps you need to be thinking about something completely different. This brings us nicely to the next chapter – Desperate Measures.

SUMMARY

Many firms fail at skills recruiting simply because they can't deliver the application it needs. Resources and the correct use of resources are key components of application.

11

Desperate Measures

TAKING STOCK

You are now at the point where you have sourced the market properly yet you are still drawing a blank. On the law of averages this means you are in one of two situations:

- You are not paying enough.

- You are facing genuine scarcity: the people you are looking for are in very short supply or they simply don't exist.

There is another possibility. There may be some aspect to your conditions of employment, something about what you do and the way that you do it, which puts people off. If, for example, you are involved in the handling of toxic substances this will be a disincentive to people to come and work for you. The same will apply if you have unusual and very anti-social working hours. On the whole, firms who come into these categories are rare. Furthermore, those that do are under no illusions at all as to why they find recruitment hard. The bigger difficulty for us is firms who *think* they have a problem with their conditions of employment when in fact they don't.

Scot-free and Scobley are in the foundry industry. They produce castings mainly for the automotive trade. Recently they extended their operation to seven day working by putting all works personnel on four on/four off continental shifts. This replaced the previous shift pattern which was the traditional 6–2/2–10/10–6 arrangement Mondays to Fridays only. Despite a pay increase the new shift system

Continued on next page

> was decidedly unpopular and a number of people – mainly skilled
> trades – voted with their feet and found jobs elsewhere. S & S
> advertised for replacements for their leavers but the advertisements
> failed to produce applicants of the right calibre. They tried again
> with similarly disappointing results.

S & S formed the view that their new four on/four off shift pattern was responsible for the lack of success in recruiting. Furthermore it allied with their retention experience – clearly people didn't like working these kinds of shifts and, convinced therefore they had a major problem, S & S began to consider the kind of desperate measures we will be looking at in this chapter – measures which, as we shall see, have:

* considerable cost consequences
* don't always work.

The reasons for S & S's sourcing difficulties, as it turned out, were rather more prosaic than they imagined. For a start their ads were gloriously inaccessible. On both of them the heading at the top simply read 'Foundry Personnel'. Further clues as to exactly what they were looking for were hard to find. The nearest they got to defining their needs was a bald statement to the effect that 'vacancies exist for both skilled and semi-skilled experienced foundry personnel (m/f).' Amazingly the fact the jobs were on shifts didn't get a mention at all – proof positive that the shift pattern wasn't the off-putter. Their availability wasn't too hot either, though not that many applicants actually got to test it out!

 Lesson: make sure your sourcing is right before you even start to consider desperate measures. Be warned, the road from here on is painful! Don't go along it unless you have to.

 The desperate measures we will be looking at in this chapter fall under two headings:

1. **Pay enticement.** What options are open to firms when they find they can't recruit because they can't match what applicants are looking for?

2. **Recruiting elsewhere.** What firms do when they discover the skills they want aren't available in their normal labour catchment area?

PAY ENTICEMENT

We left you slightly in the air at the end of Chapter 5 'Are you paying enough?' The gist to what we had to say was that:

- the acid test of pay competitiveness is your ability to recruit;

- if you can't recruit because you lack pay competitiveness then you need to face up to the problem and do something about it.

But what? That is the problem. What can you do if all the people coming along are demanding a pound an hour more than you can pay?

Here is where you start to enter Catch 22 territory. You have two options:

- Cough up and stand by for the back draught, ie pay the new starters what they're asking for and prepare for the outcry when the others find out.

- Target hard-to-recruit groups with pay increases rather like Gripnuts did with their cold forging setters in Chapter 5. Here of course you will be upsetting differentials including skilled differentials (prepare yourself for another kind of outcry).

Understandably practitioners don't like playing jiggery pokery with pay structures. If their hand is forced they will explain away their actions as 'having to bow to market forces' but they still don't feel very comfortable about it. Worse too is the fact that tampering with pay scales can set off a whole new round of dissatisfactions which, sooner or later, will escalate into an increase in staff turnover somewhere along the line. In short, the remedies become self defeating and businesses can find themselves in worse situations than they had been in the first place.

At this juncture we want to introduce an important distinction. There is a world of difference, measurable in pounds, between being competitive and having the ability to entice. Pay enticement in its simplest form is the traditional preserve of smaller firms who don't have too much to worry about in terms of structures and pay differentials (witness how Maurice Phelps enticed George Ashworth the toolmaker back in Chapter 5).

Larger employers are always going to have difficulty with pay enticement – the not-too-subtle art of making people offers they can't refuse.

So where do we go from here?

'Golden Hellos'

One device which appeared on the scene a few years ago was the so-called 'golden hello'. We have laid claim to inventing the golden hello although we are happy to admit that a number of other people in recruitment came up with the idea at about the same time.

A golden hello is an up-front payment in cash made to a new starter. It is an incentive to someone to take a new job where the salary on offer is not so much different from the salary he/she is already receiving.

Golden hellos are more normally associated with management appointments but they can and have been used on the scarce skills recruiting scene. Because it is a one-off payment, the golden hello doesn't interfere in any way with pay rates and pay structures and as such it is a convenient way round the problem posed by lack of pay competitiveness. If desperate measures means recruiting people who have been diagnosed as very scarce then enticement in the form of a golden hello may well be the name of the game you have no alternative other than to play.

Practitioners get very jumpy about golden hellos and we can understand this. The idea of making a big up-front payment to someone, particularly if that someone happens to be someone on the shop floor, certainly takes some getting used to. But there are practical objections too and these we need to look at.

Leavers

What happens if the recipients of golden hellos decide to quit? What happens if you decide to give them the sack because they prove to be unsatisfactory? How do you get your money back? Or is it a case of having to kiss your money goodbye?

Paying a golden hello against an agreement that the firm can recoup the lot (or a diminishing proportion) if the employment terminates for any reason is one approach. On the plus side the very existence of such an agreement could serve to deter the kind of person who had no intention other than pocketing the cash and moving on. But on the negative side:

- you're still left with the problem of getting the money back;

- it rather takes the gloss off the golden hello and reduces its enticement appeal.

A way round this problem is to stagger the payment over a series of instalments – say after one, three and six months. It dilutes the enticement, true, although in the case of high earners, spreading the payment over two tax periods might serve to keep them out of higher tax brackets.

Other employees

Won't golden hellos still give you problems with existing employees? Won't they still view it as unfair on them ('We didn't get £500 when we started')?

The answer is yes, probably, and we are certainly not suggesting that golden hellos should be paid furtively. These things have a habit of coming to light and look ten times worse because they have been concealed.

Golden hellos, however, have the edge over simply paying people higher wages insofar as they are a one-off event. There isn't a constant reminder of the firm's inconsistent treatment of people in the shape of the weekly or monthly pay packet.

And why not just be up-front about golden hellos? Why not say it's the only way you have to recruit people without throwing the pay structure into chaos. Make a virtue of what you're doing.

Still not happy?

We did warn you this was going to be painful.

RECRUITING IN OTHER AREAS

During the great skills shortage which accompanied the 1986–1988 boom period, it became semi-fashionable for firms from the south to embark on recruitment drives in areas which they imagined to have surpluses of skills. Typically they targeted areas of high unemployment – in the north, Scotland and in Northern Ireland. Some even went further afield, for example into EC countries where they believed there might be a greater abundance of skills.

Another phenomenon of the 80s was the firm who moved into a development area with the assistance of grants. All was hunky-dory until they realised that these areas didn't have any skills base except in traditional industries where the skills were not transferable.

Again it became necessary to try to recruit skilled people from other (industrial) areas.

There is nothing new about the fact that people in general are not a very mobile commodity and stagnation in the housing market hasn't helped mobility either. This is another factor we need to take account of. In fairness to the firms who embark on these out-of-area recruitment drives, most of them know that they will have a fairly low success rate.

Two forces govern people's attitudes to geographical relocation:

- *push:* from areas people want to quit typically because they've got high unemployment rates or because they're crime ridden. Recently there has been a push of people from areas where rented accommodation is hard to find or very expensive.

- *pull:* to areas which have something to offer, notably, of course, jobs. 'Nice places to live' (eg seaside towns) exert considerable pull force.

Selecting Target Areas

The first problem you hit is deciding where to stage your recruiting exercise; which areas to choose.

Understandably – and as we have already mentioned – a lot of firms target areas of high unemployment, areas where, on the face of it, the push forces are going to be greatest.

Two snags attached to recruiting in areas of high unemployment are:

- they may not have the right skills base and this is something you tend to discover only when you've got there. A lot of high unemployment areas are associated with diminished traditional industries, eg shipbuilding, steel making, coal mining. There will be skilled people in these areas and skilled people out of work – but they won't necessarily have the kind of skills you are looking for. The extent to which these skills are transferable (with retraining) is something for you to judge – and the government of course offers assistance with the provision of opportunities to long-term unemployed people;

- people have their roots in these areas; families, extended families, going back for many generations. The push forces may not be as strong as you think.

But why not target areas which *do* have the right skills base; where the kind of people you want exist in relative abundance? Why not indeed? This is why we see a lot of firms from the south of England advertising for skilled engineering workers in the Birmingham local papers. The problem? There are umpteen Birmingham firms advertising for the same kinds of people too. Push forces are minimal.

In shortlisting areas to target for out of town recruiting exercises we suggest you work your way through the following checklist:

- The skills base. Where are the skills you require going to be found; in which areas? If some of these areas happen to be areas with poor employment prospects then so much the better – but don't let high unemployment levels over-influence your choice. Location of competitors might help you to identify suitable areas.

- You will now have a shortlist to which you can apply a bit of push and pull analysis. Why should people want to leave these areas? What is there about your area which might attract them? Is there any thread of common interest here? Midlanders, for example, live in the most land-locked part of the country. A pull force therefore could be a job by the sea.

- If you still have a list of possible target areas and need to pick one then go for the simple expediency of choosing the nearest. Reasons?

  - Resistance to relocation increases with distance. The further removed people are from their family and friends the harder the decision will be for them.

  - The world is shrinking. Roads get better, cars get more reliable and attitudes to commuting change. In short, relocation may not even be necessary.

Sourcing

Having selected a target area you may find you don't know it too well.

You will remember our model approach to sourcing skilled people was based on *accessible* newspaper advertising. Therefore the first problem if you're recruiting in strange territory could be which newspaper to choose. Your advertising agent may be able to help you here but do be careful to check that your contact isn't simply looking through a trade directory. Your ad could end up in a completely inappropriate newspaper such as a morning paper of the sort that is normally read by business and professional people, or a freesheet which doesn't carry much recruitment advertising. If you feel your advertising agent's knowledge is suspect or if you don't have an advertising agent then fish for local contacts. People in Job Centres can be very helpful. (There are other reasons why talking to the local Job Centre is a good idea – as we shall see later.)

Having identified the appropriate newspaper the next thing you need to know is which night is job night. A quick phone call to the paper's telesales department will tell you this – at the same time you could ask them to send you a copy of the last job night edition. This will give you an idea of what the competition for labour in the area is like and whether the advertising is mostly of a display or lineage character.

When you write your ad copy, it should contain some information on the area you are located in – stressing any benefits (pull factors). If you intend to offer a relocation package then say so, ie don't leave this out or people will assume they have to fund their own relocation.

Dimflick make light switches. Recently Dimflick relocated its business from Birmingham to a greenfield site in a pleasant part of mid-Wales. Their move was grant assisted.

Dimflick employ a number of skilled people particularly in their toolroom, development and maintenance areas – and also in their primary production processes which are presswork and plastic injection moulding. Acutely aware that one of the problems in Wales will be skills shortages, Dimflick made a determined effort to move as many of their Birmingham skilled people with them as possible.

The response to this effort was disappointing. The overwhelming
Continued on next page

majority opted to stay in Birmingham and took redundancy. About 10 per cent said yes and this, Dimflick reasoned to themselves, gave them at least a core of skilled people on which to build.

With the move to Wales completed Dimflick found their problems had just begun. Recruiting skilled people locally proved even harder than they thought. To make matters worse, some of their ex-Birmingham people started to drift back. Faced with an imminent crisis Dimflick's management decided to invest in a big recruitment drive targeting Birmingham because:

- it was the nearest large industrial area;

- it was an area they knew. In particular they knew the skills they needed were available in Birmingham.

Dimflick placed an advertisement in the *Birmingham Evening Mail*. Taking on board all the points about availability they advertised:

- a phone-in line to their personnel office open till 8pm on two consecutive evenings;

- an all-day factory open event on the Saturday following the ad;

- the facility to write in if that's what applicants preferred.

The response to the open event was the most disappointing with just two not very suitable people attending. This was more the pity because Dimflick had laid on refreshments and personnel to take people on tours of the factory. On the other hand the phone-in line did quite well with 20 calls logged. Several written applications were also received – some of which looked promising.

Perhaps it seems obvious that open events, even if they are held on a Saturday, don't have much to offer in the way of availability if they are separated from the people they are targeting by 80 or 90 miles of twisting narrow roads. The virtue of using open sessions to source skilled people lies in their availability, hence there is little point to them when sourcing out of area. Phone-in lines are of course still a good tool and – if you are sourcing in an area of high unemployment – the Job Centre may be the best second string. There are three reasons for this:

- In areas of high unemployment the people you are targeting may themselves be unemployed, hence the availability problem posed by Job Centre hours doesn't apply.

- The people you are targeting may also be participants in Job

Centre activities such as job clubs. They may visit the Job Centre regularly and may have struck up a rapport with the Job Centre staff.

• Job Centre staff may be able to help you in other directions. They will have local knowledge (eg which is the best newspaper to advertise in or contact with the human resources manager in a company where there are redundancies). When you come to do interviews they may be able to provide you with free of charge facilities too – all very useful.

Conversion

Back to our case study. We left Dimflick with around 30 applicants sourced by phone-in and from people who wrote in. Let's see what happened next.

Interviews were set up for all the people who phoned in (with two exceptions – callers who clearly didn't have the right kind of experience). The suitable people who wrote in were all contacted by telephone. The interviews in every case were at times to suit the applicant which meant that most were after hours or on a Saturday which the HR officer and the factory manager set aside specially. All interviews were confirmed in writing with a 'how to find us' map.

In the event about half the interviews were cancelled or the people failed to show up. However, those that did attend were of good quality and Dimflick felt happy to offer jobs to seven people (which by then was roughly half the number of vacancies). Of these seven two declined, two accepted then declined before starting and one didn't show up on the first morning. For all their effort Dimflick got just two starters. There was further gnashing of teeth when one of these left within six weeks. What went wrong?

At the post-mortem which followed there was general agreement that spouses' jobs and the problems associated with buying and selling houses accounted for most of the candidate fall out Dimflick experienced. This prompted the managing director to suggest that they ought to target single people next time they advertised. Single people would also be easier and cheaper to relocate.

Practitioners who have been involved in relocating people in the under £20k per annum bracket know to their cost never to underestimate the problems. At the conversion point (applicants to starters) the problems in the skilled sector seem to have one or other of the following root causes:

- Some people apply who haven't really thought things through at all. Applying for jobs in other areas has an escapist appeal and for some, applying is as far as they really want to go. These kind of people tend to duck out pre-interview.

- Some people seem to get last minute cold feet about attending the interview simply because it's a long way to go – and of course there's a cost (not all firms reimburse travelling expenses). These people don't show up either.

- Some people (married people or people in permanent relationships) apply without telling their spouse or partners. The fall out occurs when their partners find out and object to being frogmarched off to live in another part of the country.

- For the most part relocation packages are inadequate. Special deals may be struck with senior executives who are being relocated but those in manual jobs are usually stuck with the rations. Some firms recruiting out of area don't even offer relocation packages at all.

- A lot of firms prefer to stay 'hands-off' when it comes to buying and selling houses. 'That's your business' is the frequent line fed out to candidates, 'We don't want to get involved.'

Some firms are good at relocating people – the usual reason being they do a lot of it. What you will tend to find in such firms is that relocation is properly thought out and properly resourced, meaning:

- there is a lot of pre-relocation input;

- cost of relocation is dealt with flexibly and on a total compensation basis. Individual circumstances are taken into account. There is no such thing as 'rations' when it comes to relocation packages;

- there is involvement in the purchase and disposal of property. This may extend to the use of professional relocation specialists – firms who are connected to estate agents or chains of estate agents. Here part of the deal might be purchasing the old property via the relocation service provider at a price determined by best of three valuations. If the property finally sells for more then the surplus goes to the relocated employee; if it sells for less then the firm picks up the tab. The beauty to this arrangement is that it removes one of the commonest causes for relocation failing. Also, if we want to be rather more cynical, it cuts off the relocated employee's route of return.

We have written this book with line managers and human resources practitioners in normal run-of-the-mill companies in mind and we realise that in most cases the kind of involvement in the relocation process we have just described will be out of their reach because they won't be sufficiently resourced in terms of money or professional staff. Normal run-of-the-mill companies may use relocation service providers from time to time but this will tend to be for:

- senior people;

- existing employees who are relocating from one company operating site to another.

So, given modest relocation resources, is there anything firms can do to cut down on the high fall out rate associated with recruiting in other areas?

Despite all we said about conversion and the need to compress selection procedures we are now going to suggest something which on the face of it sounds like doing the precise opposite. With out of area recruiting we recommend you do two separate interviews. First of all we suggest you set up preliminary interviews with the candidates you source and hold these interviews locally – local, that is, to the candidates (in your target area). You need to carry out these interviews quickly (soon after the appearance of your ad) and you need to take into account availability (making provisions to see people out of hours.) Apart from the normal employment interview pattern these interviews will also embrace the following:

- An examination of the candidate's commitment to the idea of relocation. (Why are you applying for a job with us? Why not look for something in your own town?) Watch out for vague, poorly thought-out answers. Also watch out for 'halo effects' creeping in: your liking of a candidate could tempt you to dismiss unsatisfactory answers.

- An examination of the candidate's domestic circumstances. (Will there be property to sell? Is there a spouse, partner or dependent relative? Does that person have a job? How important is that job (a) to the person and (b) to the household budget? Does the spouse/partner/dependant know the candidate is applying for a job which will mean relocation? If not, why not?)

- Information on the relocation package (prepare a handout with this set out in writing and give the candidate a copy). Explain each item and deal with any questions.

The interview should be on the basis of a full and frank exchange of information meaning the tone you set with candidates is important. You have not got to let candidates feel awkward about backing out. At the end of your preliminary interviews suggest to candidates they go away and think things over. Where there are spouses/partners/dependants suggest they, too, should be involved in the process. Unless you feel the candidate is completely unsuitable close the interview by saying the next stage will be an interview at the plant. Agree a time and date if necessary but tell candidates you will phone them first to confirm whether:

- they are still interested
- they will be attending.

Admittedly this preliminary vetting isn't foolproof but it should enable you to wheedle out a lot of people who are going to fall by the wayside anyway, ie it shifts the fall out into the earlier stages of selection, thus saving time.

Naturally you will get a better turn-up rate if you do your preliminary interviews in your target area but this can be good and bad. Good if it means you get to see people who are put off by having to go a long way for what they might see as just a first interview. Bad if it brings in timewasters and dreamers.

Suitable venues for interview

What about choice of venues for your preliminary interviews?
Job Centres are normally more than happy to provide

employers with interviewing facilities free of charge though you may have to make do with a table and two chairs in an open plan office or in the Job Centre itself.

The downside with Job Centres is, of course, their opening hours. You won't be able to run your preliminary interviews on into the evening which, unless you happen to be recruiting in an area of high unemployment, will prove a major stumbling block. This is why most firms involved in out of town recruiting exercises end up using hotels.

Two words of warning about hotels:

- Avoid posh hotels. Your interviewees could well be people who are on their way home from work; people who have been doing a manual job all day and are still in their working clothes. Not only will they feel uncomfortable (and possibly intimidated/put off) but you may start to get complaints from the hotel management (it has happened!). You won't want to have to deal with complaints when you are trying to get on with your interviews.

- When arranging interviewing facilities with hotels make it clear when you will be arriving and when you will be leaving, giving yourself a good 30 minutes leeway at either end (time to set up and time if your interviews happen to overrun). Don't get in the position where the hotel staff are banging on the door at six o'clock because the room you're in has to be converted back into a bedroom for overnight letting! Often hotels who let out interview rooms don't expect users to be running on into the evening.

Final Interviews

Let's now move on to second (and final) interviews. These will be held on site and will involve the applicants who have come through your first interview stage.

Involvement of partners/spouses/dependants in the selection process (ie anyone who might throw a spanner in the works) is all-important and it may be a good idea to suggest that whoever this person might be accompanies the candidate to the second, on-site interview. This will give you an opportunity to discuss relocation issues with both parties present.

'A long way to go for just a first interview' is a frequently given reason for cancelling or not turning up to interviews in far-flung places. 'Is it worth it?' 'Is there that much chance of getting the job?' And this is where candidates start writing themselves off before they even start. Remember that a lot of skilled candidates have had bad experiences with employers and interviews, notably:

- employers who have put them through processions of interviews then still said no;

- attending interviews and then hearing nothing (a bad mannered way of telling candidates they've not been successful or the job isn't available any more).

The fact that the first interview on site is a final interview will help you to overcome some of these misgivings. Candidates feel they are already some way along the road to getting the job. It also helps to assure candidates that the final interview really *is* the final interview and that they will know the outcome within a few (say how many) days. The fear that applying for the job could turn into a kind of endurance test involving several long trips is taken away.

The cost of getting to the interview is the other item that concerns candidates. What is surprising here is:

- the number of firms who don't pay travelling expenses;

- the number of firms who do but don't say so until the interview;

- (worst of all) the number of firms who only pay travelling expenses to candidates who ask.

Candidates need to be told pre-interview that their travelling expenses will be reimbursed. You can do this at the preliminary interview or when you speak to them on the phone to confirm they will be coming to the interview, or preferably on both occasions. Confirming the time and date of their second interview by letter also helps.

Finally, on the subject of minimising fall out at the second (on site) interview stage, take a leaf out of Dimflick's book and send your candidates a 'How to find us' pack – or at least a clear set of directions and a location map. Candidates do get lost in strange areas but the difficulty arises when they realise they are going to be late. Feeling they've blown it they tend to turn round and go home.

Start Dates

Earlier in the book we looked at notice periods for skilled people and how extending them might be used as a retention device.

Most skilled people are still subject to one week's notice though the incidence of people on monthly terms is increasing. Hence skilled people to whom you offer jobs (those that accept) will tend to be joining you pretty quickly and with people involved in relocation, this can cause a problem in itself. In our experience a lot of post interview/pre-employment fall out occurs for the simple reason that the people concerned feel things are moving too fast for them. If you get people changing their minds at the last minute then it might be worthwhile ringing them up to find out why. Be prepared in these situations to offer to put back starting dates. There is a risk, of course, that the reasons you are being given are not the full reasons. Your new starter may, for instance, be having reluctant spouse problems which more time may not help to resolve. You will come to the point where enough is enough.

With relocating employees the potential problems don't end with someone starting the new job. There may still be property to buy and property to sell and families to be relocated. During this settling-in period the more open doors there are the better.

Measuring success when recruiting skilled people in other areas requires a different yardstick from the one you use for local recruiting. Conversion and retention beyond the short term are particularly difficult and you should not be too disappointed if your efforts show a meagre return.

What about Dimflick? Do we have any further advice for them – apart from selling up and going back to Birmingham?

The problems of companies in areas which don't have a skills base are problems which don't go away. Importing skills (relocating skilled people) will only ever nibble away at the edges of these problems – and the cost and pain should never be underestimated. What Dimflick clearly need to do as a matter of urgency is to get their training act together (apprenticeships). This won't help them in the short term but three to four years hence they will have a crop of young skilled people coming onstream. Perhaps also they need to front load their apprentice-ships, eg have a double intake in the first couple of years. Training isn't without a cost but it's far cheaper than having to recruit out of area every time you have a skilled vacancy. More on this subject in Chapter 15.

A final word here about extending the search for skilled people even further afield and recruiting from overseas. The advent of free movement of labour within the European Com-munity has raised recruitment of overseas nationals to the level of an issue for serious consideration in a lot of firms who would previously never have even entertained the idea.

Overseas nationals do figure in the skilled sector but in the main they are people who have found their own way here. Firms who have actually recruited skilled people from overseas are still few and far between. The sources most frequently used are:

- networks – engineering approaches via existing employees who are overseas nationals (friends and family back home);

- (with multinationals) using an overseas-based associate company to carry out recruitment.

Verdict on carrying out recruitment exercises overseas: they are fraught with the same kind of problems as recruiting in other areas – only worse. Certainly not one for the uninitiated.

RELOCATING BUSINESSES

An alternative to relocating skilled people to where you are is to turn the tables and relocate the business to where the skills are available. This is, of course, real desperate measures stuff and should not be contemplated unless all other options have been exhausted (possibly the measure of very last resort).

Just two thoughts on relocating businesses:

- If you need to relocate the business anyway (eg premises too small, lease expired etc) then take account of skills avail-ability. Don't do a Dimflick and go for wherever the grants happen to be biggest hoping skills provision will take care of itself (it won't and it will be a bugbear to you for a very long time).

- If you are in a skills-starved area don't relocate the business locally for no better reason than it's where the key management people happen to live. Relocating a handful of managers or having them commute further could be a far less expensive option than having the ongoing problem of skills shortages and recruiting out of area. Never underestimate this cost.

Recruiting out of area for jobs out of area

This has got nothing to do with desperate measures but we wanted to acknowledge at this point that firms recruiting out of area are not always seeking to relocate people.

An example that springs to mind is the firm with a field service network seeking to recruit a service engineer to cover a territory – where the person they want to take on would need to be resident within the territory.

SUMMARY

Only use desperate measures if you have to. Even then, think twice.

12

Alternative Solutions to Skills Shortages

What do firms do when they think they've tried everything? What do firms do when they don't like the sound of desperate measures? In this chapter we want to look at two rather unusual approaches to skills shortages:

- using retired people; and

- tapping into the moonlight economy.

We want to look at what these approaches have to offer and how – with a bit of refinement – they can be used at least as stopgap measures.

RECRUITING RETIRED PEOPLE

Recruiting people who have officially retired may not seem an obvious answer to helping offset skills shortages. But this is precisely what some firms have done and, on the whole, they don't seem displeased with the result.

Retired people fall into two categories:

- existing employees who agree to work on after normal retiring age;

- retired people recruited on the outside market.

There are pros and cons to employing over 65s. On the plus side there is experience and perhaps the qualities which go with being one of the old school – responsibility, dependability and that kind of thing. There's also the fact that over 65s don't have much in the way of employment rights which will be seen as an advantage by some employers.

For the negatives, let's ask some of our practitioners what they think:

'People don't want to work on after they retire. All they want to do is pack up.'

True to an extent but in many cases the urge to find a job arises not at the point of retirement but six to twelve months later. Whether this is just a case of feeling bored or missing old routines is hard to say. But what mustn't be discounted is the fact that a lot of pensioners these days can start to find themselves hard up. Fragmented employment in the later years of working life can, as we know, have a dire effect on occupational pensions and sadly we have seen a lot of fragmented employment in our recession plagued recent past. People retiring with long service and good pensions (manual workers) are becoming quite rare birds. Thus the need to find work is often driven by financial necessity. Either that or give up luxuries.

'Pensioners don't want to work full time.'

Again this is true to an extent but not something you should take for granted. Pre-1986 there was a ceiling on what over 65s could earn without incurring a pound for pound reduction in their state pensions. The ceiling figure less 1p divided by the hourly rate for the job tended to determine how many hours a pensioner wanted to work. This doesn't apply any more so pensioners are less averse to the idea of full-time work than they used to be. On the whole though part-time work is still preferred.

'Old people are prone to more health problems than young people. They have more time off.'

When this view is expressed it is usually and immediately challenged. Firms with experience of employing over 65s are almost unanimous in the view that pensioner workers have better attendance records than their younger counterparts. Health problems, when they do arise, tend to be of a more serious and long-term nature. In these situations the decision to 'call it a day' often comes from the employees themselves. Furthermore if it is necessary to have to terminate the employment of an over 65 on health grounds there are no employment rights and accordingly no potential litigation to worry about as would be the case with a younger person.

'Old people's skills are obsolete. They're no use in modern manufacturing and engineering environments.'

This hardly makes sense in the case of people who have just retired, people who are working on after normal retirement age. In any case lack of new technology skills tends to have more to do with previous employment than age. If a person has been working for a number of years in a firm where investment levels have been poor and where equipment and methods are antiquated then yes, that person will have skills which are obsolete. Yet there are a lot of young people who fall into this category too.

'Keeping pensioners on is bad for young people. It blocks off their avenues of promotion and prevents skills succession.'

There is something in this argument. If, for example, you have a skilled production team which consists of one team leader on a higher rate than the others and if that team leader is allowed to stay on after retiring age then this will have an obvious and demoralising effect on ambitious younger members of the team. It could be a good enough reason for some of them to decide to leave. What you clearly need to do is ensure that over 65s working on don't block other people's promotion paths. This, as a rule, means barring them from supervisory and management jobs. By and large, however, most skilled workers staying on won't be in supervisory or management jobs, hence they won't be blocking anyone's promotion routes.

Skills succession, the handing on of skills from older to younger workers, could also suffer if there is no finite point at which older workers retire. For instance if Sam, who programmes the wire eroder, is sixty-four and a half and he knows he is retiring at sixty-five he will be more likely to pass on his know-how to Dave who works with him. If he is planning on staying on after 65 and if the management is agreeable to this, he will be more inclined to keep his knowledge to himself. Dave will therefore suffer.

Again this is an area of genuine concern which can only be resolved by ensuring in these situations that skills succession is management rather than employee controlled. Hence teaching Dave to programme the wire eroder will feature in Sam's job instructions and Dave's progress will be monitored.

Concern for younger employees and how they view their

future prospects is the reason why many companies have gone for a compulsory and unwaivable retirement age.

Using retirees is perhaps best conceived as a stopgap measure; a solution to skills shortages in the shorter term rather than something you want to do on an ongoing basis. It will appeal, for example, to firms whose needs are in the short term (eg completion of a big contract). It will also appeal to firms who are setting up apprentice training programmes but who need a skilled workforce to bridge the gap while people in training are coming onstream.

Here is a list of points you will need to consider before embarking on recruiting over 65s.

- Do you have a compulsory retirement age? If so, you will need to get rid of it.

- What scope do you have for part-time employment in skilled areas? If you can offer part-time work for over 65s then this will attract more applicants. In viewing the possibility of breaking down skilled jobs into part-time hours look for real rather than perceived difficulties. A real difficulty would, for example, be with a service engineer who is visiting customers' premises all day. Having two people doing four hour stints would be very disruptive, involving additional journeys to and from base.

- Run through your terms and conditions of employment and root out any clauses which might put off over 65s. A favourite here is entitlement to company sickness benefits. Often over 65s are not included. The fear in this case (that older people have more time off) is not well founded. Aim at harmonising conditions of employment irrespective of age. Try to make employment an attractive prospect for people over retiring age.

- Introduce pre-retirement counselling or extend existing pre-retirement counselling to include discussion of staying on. Signal the company position on staying on – particularly important if you have previously had a compulsory retirement policy.

- Look at the rules of your pension scheme. Is there a facility for deferring pensions? Continuing to contribute after 65 and thereby enhancing their eventual pension could be an attractive prospect for people with fragmented employment in their latter years – people whose occupational pensions will have suffered in the process.

- Don't take people in supervisory and management jobs entirely out of the reckoning. If retiring supervisors and managers are skilled (ie people who have been promoted up from the shop floor) then the idea of going back on the tools for a few years may be an inviting prospect.

Tales from the Front Line

When visiting a small firm a few years ago we came across an old acquaintance – someone we had known as the engineering manager of a big name manufacturing company up to when he retired. What was he doing? Working 20 hours a week as a bench fitter, he explained. Knowing his previous employer had serious skills shortages we asked him why he hadn't stayed on there. 'That is simple', was his reply, 'No-one asked me.'

MOONLIGHTERS

The skilled sector has traditionally depended on high levels of overtime earnings which in recessionary periods haven't been there. The restoration of overtime post-recession has in some cases been slow or incomplete and this seems to be the reason for a groundswell in the numbers of skilled people looking for nice little earners on the side.

Some industries operate weekend shifts and it is not unusual to find the skilled component to these shifts made up of people with normal 39 hour Monday to Friday jobs.

Again, the skilled component to twilight (part-time evening) shifts is often provided by people who have jobs elsewhere.

Mainstream employers tend to view moonlighters with an element of hostility tinged with suspicion, the main areas of reservation being:

- as a rule moonlighters are looking for evening or weekend work (unless they happen to be shiftworkers), ie most of them won't be available when you want them;

- how can anyone be fresh who's just finished an eight hour shift somewhere else?

- moonlighters are looking for cash in hand work. Firms who insist on making the proper tax and national insurance deductions hold no interest for them (not necessarily true by the way).

Clearly you need to decide if you can use moonlighters and, indeed, whether you want to. In skills-intensive industries (high proportion of the total labour force is skilled) you may stand a better chance of manning a shift if you run it at weekends (enabling you to use moonlighters) than if, for example, you moved single shift (normal days) into double shifts (6–2/2–10) working.

SUMMARY

When skills shortages are acute be flexible about who you employ and the hours you ask them to work. Be prepared if necessary to adapt working hours to the people who are available.

13

Trouble Shooting

We have devoted much of this book to showing you how you can recruit people with scarce skills if you use the right methods and – in particular – if you pay attention to our 3 As: *accessibility, availability* and *application*. Conversely if you use the wrong recruiting methods you can create artificial skills shortages for yourself and in our work we see this happening time and time again.

There are instances, however, of firms who do use the right recruiting methods and who still find themselves in difficulty – and the reasons are not immediately obvious. The temptation for them is to move onto the kind of desperate measures we have been looking at in the last two chapters when in fact this isn't necessary.

SKILLS WHICH DON'T EXIST

In our first chapter we looked at how employers bring skills shortages on themselves by tightening up skills specifications. We gave the example of a modern manufacturing business recruiting maintenance engineers. Here the specification had been upgraded to include a complexity of electrical and mechanical skills. By definition, with each upgrading the pool of potential applicants gets smaller and smaller.

Overspecification, carrying this process to the extreme, is a phenomenon we have witnessed several times in the last few years – in effect firms seeking to recruit people who don't exist or who only exist in very small numbers (the range of skills in question having, in many cases, been acquired purely by chance).

What causes firms to overspecify?

- **Replacing a leaver:** old George is retiring, old George has been with the firm 25 years, old George can turn his hand to practically anything – hence what we need is an exact replica of old George and his skills (old George is probably unique).

- **Reduced manning levels:** job holders expected to carry out wide ranges of tasks previously done by a number of people.

- **Emergence of more small firms/fragmentation of large ones:** people in small units are as a natural consequence expected to carry out a wider range of functions.

- **Skills enhancement:** firms seeking to recruit people who are of a better standard than their current workforce.

Tell-tale signs of overspecifying are large numbers of applicants diagnosed as 'not suitable', ie the 'can't recruit' problem isn't down to sourcing or conversion; it's simply that no-one comes up to scratch. What happens in these situations? The firm of course readvertises, usually warning previous applicants not to reapply, and the same thing happens again. The point to realising you are overspecifying is that no amount of accessibility, availability and application is going to help you. You need to take stock and see what the market is telling you about the kinds of people who are available.

MOVING THE GOALPOSTS

This is a problem which isn't peculiar to the skilled sector.

Firms are sometimes in the habit of altering their specifications during the selection process. They start by trying to recruit someone with a particular set of skills and competencies then, later on, they start introducing refinements or new sets of skills and competencies altogether. The clue to this phenomenon is when the applicants look OK at first stage then get turned down at final interview. If you like, this is candidate fall out which is employer-induced.

In a typical manufacturing business the common cause of

shifting specifications is a failure in communication between line management (who do the final selection) and the human resources department (who do the sourcing and preliminary sifting). The former provide the latter with insufficient or insufficiently clear information on what they need. The latter (who tend to be generalists) may not be too clear about the nitty gritty anyway.

Long drawn-out selection procedures are another cause of shifting specifications. Circumstances change over a period of time and job specifications become subject to modification (naturally). Shifting specifications are at the root of many firms' recruiting difficulties.

SELECTION TESTS

This section is aimed at those firms which use selection tests.

Our biggest argument with tests so far has been where they become a reason for selection procedures extending. Having to come back on a separate occasion for a selection test (happens a lot) invites candidate fall out. If the test has to be conducted in normal office hours (also happens a lot) this invites further fall out. It will help you therefore if you can do your tests at the same time as your interviews and if you can do both at times which suit candidates (availability).

Tests, as we know, come in all shape and sizes. A major concern is where a significant number of hard-sourced candidates 'fail' the test. In fairness the case-lore here tends to centre round homespun tests (tests companies design themselves) yet with all tests, not just bad tests, there is a need for alarm bells to sound if 'not enough candidates are passing the test' is the reason you can't recruit. With skilled people the evidence they can do the job is in any case in their previous employment hence aptitude type tests are largely a waste of space. If you feel tests are achieving nothing except getting in the way of your skills recruiting then don't use them. The kind of tests that are 'company policy' need particular scrutiny.

SKILLS WHICH HAVE DIED OUT

There is such a thing as genuine skills scarcity. No amount of accessibility, availability and application will alleviate genuine skills scarcity for you – the simple fact is that the people aren't there. The important thing about genuine skills scarcity is to recognise it – to know when you are flogging a dead horse.

Genuine skills scarcity is sometimes a local phenomenon. Sometimes it is more widespread.

How does genuine skills scarcity arise?

- A skill can become obsolete because of changed circumstances in the industry which spawned it. Notably, new technology can render a skill obsolete. The problem then arises for firms who are still using the old technology and the old skills. The difficulty is compounded by the fact that bigger firms will tend to acquire new technology before smaller firms, and bigger firms are usually the providers of training in an industry. Once they cease to train people in a skill, the trade declines and the small firms are left with the skills shortage.

- The providers of training in an industry get wiped out because of recession or they cease to be providers of training anymore. The depletion of foundry skills in the West Midlands can be attributed to the disappearance of some of the leading names in training.

- Working practices change, rendering skills obsolete. The example of the multi-skilled maintenance engineer serves to illustrate this point. Previously maintenance departments in factories were filled with all sorts of odd trades, eg pipefitters, guard makers, etc. Often these trades were protected by rigorously enforced demarcation practices. Today job definitions and demarcation practices have largely been wiped away. Hence anyone trying to recruit a guard maker these days might have some difficulty.

Apart from training your own people, ways out of genuine skills scarcities are rather limited. Enticement of what skills are available is one option and this is where devices like golden hellos can start to come into their own. There is also the possibility that the skill which is so scarce in your neck of the woods might be available in greater abundance somewhere else – over to recruiting out of area.

A far easier route, though, for many firms is to take stock of what they are doing and to see if the skills scarcity problem can be cracked by approaching it from a different direction. Here are two examples:

- Using our old-fashioned maintenance department again, we could stop looking for a guard maker and instead set the specification for one of the new breed of maintenance engineers. With a department full of such characters any one of them should be able to turn their hands to making guards. However this will mean shaking out the working practices first.

- Some skills are very transferable – from one industry to another. For example someone who can make die sets used in the die-casting industry will have no problem transferring onto plastic injection moulds. In an area where plastic injection moulders are plentiful and die casters are thin on the ground, the latter could gain enormously by opening themselves to applications from people with either/or experience.

SUMMARY

Make sure *you* are not the cause of your skills shortages.

14

Employment Packages for Skilled People

One group who can be said to have benefited greatly from skills shortages is skilled people themselves. Not only has competition for their services caused rates of pay to go up in leaps and bounds but firms have gone out of their way to make themselves more attractive to skilled people by providing enhanced terms and conditions of employment packages. A notable development has been the extension of staff status to groups of skilled workers. Companies have seen staff status as an aid to both retention and recruitment.

STAFF STATUS – WHAT DOES IT MEAN?

Over the years there has been a general move towards harmonising white and blue collar conditions of employment. Hence what used to be cherished staff perks now tend to be benefits enjoyed by all. Elevating a group of people onto staff status hasn't, therefore, got the same magic connotations it used to have. As a typical example, in a case we dealt with recently the main gains were:

- better sick pay – full salary for three months as opposed to basic SSP;

- full salary in lay-offs or periods of short time as opposed to statutory guarantee payments;

- membership of the staff pension scheme (better benefits but higher contributions too);

- long service holidays – an extra day's holiday with every five years' service up to a maximum of five;

- not having to clock in or clock out.

How Staff Status can go Wrong

Hotpots Holloware Products completed a staff status deal with its skilled employees. It was felt that staff status would go some way towards reducing labour turnover in skilled areas and that it would serve as an aid to recruitment too.

Three important features of the deal were:
- skilled employees were no longer required to clock in or clock out;

- full salary was paid during periods of sickness as opposed to SSP only;

- there was to be no payment for overtime in line with the rest of the staff. Instead of hourly rates skilled grades were put on fixed salaries which, in annual terms, equated to their previous 39 hour pay plus a notional figure to take account of 'average' overtime earnings. It was emphasised to skilled people that they were still expected to work overtime as and when the company required.

Prior to the deal overtime had always been dealt with on a voluntary basis. If overtime was needed the company always asked for volunteers and there were usually more than enough takers. Indeed in some areas employees were regularly pestering managers for overtime to be made available.

With the advent of staff conditions all this changed. No-one wanted overtime anymore. It was seen as work without pay. Time and time again the company found itself in the position of having to detail people to work overtime on a 'you, you and you' basis. This led to a lot of bad feeling.

The other area of concern was the increase in levels of sickness absence. This was as much as 15–20 per cent and it wasn't just the cynics who made the link between increased sickness and the availability of full pay.

Continued on next page

Of course increased absenteeism (fewer pairs of hands available) introduced the need for even more overtime and the frictions developed.

All in all, after six months of staff status, Hotpots are beginning to figure they've made a big mistake. Labour turnover in skilled areas has in fact gone up – a by-product, as they see it, of all the arguing about overtime. The problem is where to go from here. Turning the clock back – reverting skilled people to hourly-paid status – seems riddled with potential pitfalls and Hotpots are beginning to rue not putting their deal onto, say, a twelve month trial basis.

Whether having their staff status deal on a twelve month trial would have helped Hotpots very much is open to debate. Trial or not, withdrawing staff privileges isn't going to go down very well and doubtless further traumas are ahead for Hotpots' team of managers.

Not all staff status deals have attracted the sort of problems Hotpots experienced. Indeed many firms who have gone down the staff status road feel they have gained.

This case study illustrates how easy it is for staff status deals to become self defeating. What starts out as an honest attempt at improving the lot of skilled workers (to help retain and recruit them) ends up as a reason for some of them leaving.

On reflection the sad truth about Hotpots is that both their management people and their skilled workers were really far happier with hourly rates. Managers got people to work overtime without having to resort to coercion; skilled workers got paid for the time they put in. The conditions which prevailed after staff status were to no-one's liking.

PROBATIONARY PERIODS

We want to leave staff status now and move on to what we consider to be more important matters insofar as employment packages are concerned.

Firstly let's look at probationary periods. The probationary or trial periods most firms have in their conditions of employment do seem to bother people increasingly these days.

The world of jobs has become a curious place and people applying for jobs are generally more cautious than they used to be. This includes a lot of skilled people who, by and large, are people who are looking for their job moves to provide them with permanence and progression. Coupled with this is the fact that many of their number will have had bad experiences on the job market – or they will know people who have had bad experiences. Top of the list of bad experiences at the moment seems to be jobs which turn out on closer scrutiny to be temp jobs or one of those strange 'temp to perm' arrangements which have blossomed in recent years.

In today's climate anything which suggests a job could come to an abrupt end is enough to set off alarm bells and in this respect the wording of probationary provisions in offers of employment is usually quite stark – 'this offer of employment is conditional on a satisfactory completion of a four week trial period' etc.

Recruiters don't see what all the fuss is about. They view probationary periods as part of the standard props of employment – innocuous and hardly ever invoked. Hardly worth mentioning indeed.

Getting skilled people to make job moves is all about instilling them with confidence in the organisation they may be joining and this has never been more the case than it is today. In this context we view probationary periods as potentially quite destructive – and for what real gain? Periods of notice, entitlement to written reasons for dismissal are now all items covered by statute. What you do in these respects is no longer governed by whether the employee is still in a probationary period or not.

If you're not happy about removing probationary periods across the board then what you may prefer to consider is abandoning them insofar as your scarce skills recruiting is concerned.

WORKING HOURS

We have already mentioned firms whose recruiting and retention difficulties are largely caused by the antisocial nature of the jobs they have to offer. We also mentioned that such firms are rarely under any illusion as to where their problems lie.

In the skilled sector the antisocial part to most jobs usually has something to do with the hours – either shifts or conditional overtime or having to be available for callouts etc.

What scope there is for 'humanising' hours of work and thereby improving ability to retain and recruit depends largely on the circumstances. In a lot of cases, because of the demands of customer service or continuous processes, it simply isn't possible – or firms will feel they have gone as far as they can.

However just to show it *can* be done here are a few examples.

- Permanent production night shifts organised round four long shifts (4 × 10 hour shifts Monday to Thursday only) are infinitely more popular than the 5 × 8 hour Monday to Friday variety. The three-day weekend is very appealing. Second job people, people who work weekend shifts somewhere else, can also fit into this kind of pattern, thus widening your potential recruitment catchment.

- Continuous operations can benefit from having permanent weekend shifts (people who work Friday/Saturday/Sunday) as opposed to cycling the entire workforce through seven days on one of these four on/four off continental shift patterns. With the introduction of seven day patterns there is always going to be an egress of people who don't like working weekends – and remember skilled categories are always the ones who will find it easiest to find something more to their liking on the outside market.

- People working 2–10pm shift (the 'deadman's shift' as it is known) either on a permanent or rotating basis are on the whole much happier if they can work a short shift on Friday (with the hours added on to the shifts earlier in the week).

What is interesting about these examples is that the 'humanising' is achieved with no significant increase in cost and no significant detrimental effect on the end product.

The more sociable your working hours are, the more people will want to come and work for you. People you take on will want to stay with you; they are less likely to view you as a stopgap. As a spinoff you might find also that your levels of absenteeism recede – the kind of absenteeism associated with people knocking off unpopular days.

PRESENTATION OF JOB OFFERS

A not uncommon arrangement in a lot of manufacturing companies is skilled maintenance personnel who are on callout. The factory works 24 hours but the maintenance team are based on days with the proviso that they come out when there's a breakdown to attend to.

The requirement to attend callouts is usually set out in any offer of employment. The condition itself is made clear and the arrangements for payment are described in some detail. However, what is frequently omitted from job offers is some idea of how many callouts an employee can expect to have to attend: how often the telephone will be ringing in the middle of the night.

In an example of a job offer we saw recently, the do's and don'ts of callouts took up a good half a page – about one-third of the total content of the letter. A candidate receiving such an offer could be excused for thinking that if callouts merited such detailed attention then there must be a lot of them. The truth, it turned out, was that the maintenance crew took callouts on an informal rota. Most out of hours calls could in any event be dealt with over the phone (eg by telling the night shift supervisor to throw a switch or swap production onto another machine). The average number of actual attendances worked out at about only three or four a year.

In another example we had a firm who built plant – roughly 10 per cent of which went to export customers. A condition of employment for their service engineers was that they had to be prepared to go anywhere in the world for unspecified periods and at the drop of a hat. The impression given was one of frequent, lengthy and abrupt separations from loved ones when in truth all it involved was two or three overseas trips a year, mainly to EC destinations with away-from-home times of less than five days. In fact, the firm had a net of overseas distributors who took care of most overseas work.

Such overstatements are unnecessary and misleading. In fairness to many firms though, in the past they may have had problems with people claiming this, that or the other wasn't fully explained to them when they took the job. These days of course a lot of these grouses have the habit of ending up in litigation, eg 'I had to give the job up because of so and so therefore I have been constructively dismissed'. Who can blame firms for wanting to dot every 'i' and cross every 't'?

Our plea to recruiters is to try to strike the balance. Tell it as it is *not* worse than it is. Give potential new starters the facts, good and bad, and no-one can ever blame you for that.

Overstating the negative factors in job offers normally only comes to light when someone turns the job offer down. Firms ring us up to say they can't understand it; the candidate seemed so keen at the interview. So what's the problem? Why have they changed their mind? When we relay it back to the firm that the candidate has got hold of the wrong end of the stick and that maybe the letter offering employment didn't help, the firms concerned frequently express their surprise. 'But we explained that in great detail at the interview', they say. 'We went through everything. We said there was a callout but we explained it only happened once in a blue moon.'

There are three points to remember here:

- The job offer in writing comes after the interview(s). It is the most recent information the candidate has, hence it is this which will be taken as fact.

- Anything in writing carries more weight than anything explained orally. If one thing has been said at an interview and something slightly different appears in an offer of employment then the latter will be taken as valid.

- Inconsistencies between what is said at interviews and what the firm later puts into writing in a job offer can sow seeds of doubt in candidates' minds. That essential confidence in the prospective employer is easily shattered by an unfortunate choice of words harping on the negative and conflicting with what has been said when the candidate and employer were face to face.

Going through jobs offers with successful candidates first (over the phone) as we recommend will help forestall a lot of these sorts of problems.

Offers in Writing

Please make sure you put your job offers in writing. Apart from leaving no room for misunderstanding on the contents of the offer, something in writing is, for many skilled candidates these days, an essential prerequisite to handing in notice.

We are happy to say that most firms are in no need of this particular piece of advice – they put their job offers into writing as a matter of course. But there are still a minority who draw a distinction between staff and hourly paid employees where the latter are dealt with verbally and on the shake of a hand.

Also remember not to delay sending out job offers – all part of compressing selection procedures into the minimum period of time possible and thereby enhancing your ability to convert applicants into starters.

ANTISOCIAL TERMS OF EMPLOYMENT

There will always be some companies whose terms and conditions of employment are antisocial as far as most people are concerned. Is there anything these firms can do to help them recruit and retain?

One factor in favour of most antisocial skilled jobs is that they are generally well paid: the antisocial factor has attracted a premium. There will always be people who, for one reason or another, are interested in more money. Although they still view the conditions as antisocial they will put up with them out of need.

The other factor is that what's antisocial to one person isn't necessarily antisocial to another. For example:

- **Ivor** who is a part-time schools soccer coach and who fits in his activities by working permanent nights.

- **Dev** whose wife has a shop. Working shifts means he can help her. It means he can help with looking after the kids too.

- **Ray** whose hobby is surfing. Working four on/four off continental shifts means he can get down to the coast regularly.

- **Bob** who wants to see the world before he settles down. Working as an overseas commission and installation engineer enables him to do this. He is learning some languages as well.

When employing people for jobs with unsocial conditions

success will follow if you get your sourcing right. If the right kinds of people are enquiring (eg people who put money before a cushy existence or people who see the conditions as a plus point) then they will stand a good chance of converting into starters and equally you should stand a good chance of being able to retain them too. Conversely, if 8am to 5pm type people with rigid social and domestic arrangements apply then they won't convert, or if they do come on board the chances are they will be doing so out of desperation – they need the job because they are unemployed or an axe is dangling over their necks. These are the kind of people who will view the job as a stopgap. They will be off the first chance they get and you will be agonising over why your labour turnover is going up.

You will recall that when we looked at advertising and the accessibility of advertising matter how we stressed the import-ance of including any unusual or antisocial conditions in your ad copy. Coupled with pay accessibility this has a double-barrelled function:

- it tells the kind of people you want to recruit: 'this is the job for you';

- it puts off people who won't be any use to you anyway, ie it saves on time wasting.

If you are running phone-in or open house sessions you can, in your brief description of the job, emphasise again any unsocial points. We say this because with well paid, unsocial conditions jobs you will always get some people who only see the money. Either they don't read the ad through properly or they mentally blank out the bit in the ad which describes what, in the fullness of time, they will regard as major disadvantages.

In short, *accessibility* is the key to recruiting people successfully into jobs where the conditions are slightly unusual.

SUMMARY

In reviewing employment packages for skilled people don't stop at staff status. Focus your attention on what will really help you recruit and retain people in scarce skills categories.

15

Training: The Way Back from Skills Shortages

Some people reading this book will say we have missed the point altogether. That really none of our prescriptions are solutions to skills shortages (the shrinking pool). Instead we have been putting forward ways and means of redistributing skilled people – a never-ending game in which there are always going to be losers and winners. The losers, the firms left with skills shortages, will be those who are least adept at recruiting/retaining – and those who pay the least.

We understand this criticism. However the situation employers have at the moment is a bit like the situation described by the mythical Irishman who, when asked for directions, said 'if I were you I wouldn't be starting from here'. In an ideal world we wouldn't be starting with skills shortages.

The state we're in with skilled people (and most practitioners agree that we *are* in a state) has been blamed across the board. For instance:

- Successive governments have been blamed for not paying sufficient attention to skills training; for not providing adequate initiatives or funding.

- Industry has been blamed for being short-termist and not attaching the right priorities to skills training.

- Young people themselves have been blamed for not being interested.

Which of these blame theories you espouse depends to a large extent on where you are coming from socially and politically, and what your own experiences have been.

There is general agreement, however, that the way back from skills shortages, the only way back, is if, as a nation, we can sustain adequate levels of skills training. The pool of skilled people urgently needs topping up and the future of much of manufacturing industry depends on how we succeed in doing this. Few would disagree with this view.

We acknowledged in our first chapter that one of the difficulties with the supply of skilled people is its inelasticity. Even with the best training methods in the world it takes several years to bring a skilled person onstream. So what we have had to consider – what this book has largely been about – is what employers can do in the shorter term: how to bridge the gap until training can be made to bear fruit. But in addressing this problem we are in no way suggesting our prescriptions should be viewed as a substitute for training. They are stopgaps, no more.

Earlier on in the book we looked at firms who don't have retention problems in their skilled grades – firms where the feelgood factor is high. Whether the correlation is accidental or not, we have noticed how often these firms are firms which have good apprenticeship schemes in place.

We hope that this book serves to illustrate in quite stark terms how training pays. If, every time you have a skilled vacancy, you have to go out onto a market where demand exceeds supply, if every time you have to pay big advertising bills; if the only way to succeed is by piling on the availability and application, then it paints a very bleak picture indeed for the future. Somehow and at some point you've got to get yourself off this skills shortages rack and training is the only way.

THE GOLDEN AGE OF TRAINING

We think it helps to scupper the idea which is current in some circles that back in the 50s and 60s there existed a kind of 'Golden Age' of skills training which somehow we need to get back to.

Firstly, the conditions in those years were far different from the conditions we have today, and comparisons can be unhelpful. For a start industry – the provider of training – didn't have to face the kind of global competition and consumer-dominated markets which are facts of life in the modern world. Some commentators have asked what happened to good old-fashioned altruism, ie training for training's sake. Altruism, sorry to say, goes out of the window when survival of the business is at stake.

Another factor is the fragmentation of much of manufacturing industry in recent years. Apart from large companies decent-ralising and downsizing we are living in the age of the small firm. Training is of course an activity which needs to be properly resourced and, as such, it is an activity which draws benefits from scale. Put another way, the more training you do the more cost effective it becomes. With smaller firms the logic works in reverse. Training people in ones and twos attracts the greatest unit cost to the point where some small employers will ask themselves 'is this worth it?'.

Small firms have always had a problem with training and there is nothing new about this. In fact, before anyone starts getting too sentimental about the passing of the Golden Age it pays to remember that one of the reasons we had an Industrial Training Act in 1965 with its systems of levies and grants was because not everyone was seen to be doing their fair share of training. If you are fishing for what's different about small firms today it's simply this: there are lots, lots more of them.

Verdict on going back to the Golden Age? Times have changed and in any case turning the clock back never works. In addressing training as an issue what we need to take account of is the way things are *today*.

PROVISION OF SKILLS TRAINING

In our opening chapter we identified what most practitioners would regard as being the reasons for the supply of skilled people drying up:

- the demise of the traditional apprenticeship;

- the shortage of takers for what training places *are* available.

We will be looking at the problems associated with recruiting of apprentices in a moment but what about the traditional apprenticeship?

When people talk about traditional apprenticeships it is sometimes difficult to know precisely what they mean. Before the 1965 Act, apprenticeships were largely time-based – indeed skilled people, particularly the older ones, still speak of being time served. You went into an apprenticeship at 16 years old and you came out of it at 21. What went on in between depended a lot on your firm, your boss and which particular 'Nelly' you had the good or bad luck to be told to sit by.

Most practitioners agree that training has moved on since those days. In the late 60s, largely because of the influence of the Industrial Training Boards with their powers to extort levies and award grants, skills acquisition became more competence based – a question of attaining targets by completion of specified modules (those modules which happened to be relevant to your trade). How long it took you was to a large extent neither here nor there. The same kind of approach is reflected in NVQ-based modern apprenticeships.

Going back to time-serving probably isn't what most people in industry have in mind when they talk about resurrecting traditional apprenticeships. What is really bothering them is the number of apprenticeships available today compared with the number of apprenticeships available 30 years ago. What recruiters want to see return is the *volume*.

But given this general and overwhelming consensus for more apprentice training why is it we're not seeing a massive expansion in the provision of places? This may seem harsh but could it be a case of a lot of people out there saying 'yes please' to more training, but only providing someone else is doing it?

Training, alas, is like charity. If it begins anywhere it begins at home – and expecting big firms to provide the training as it was years ago won't wash any more. In many cases the big firms of yesteryear are no longer there.

RECRUITING APPRENTICES

It is disappointing when providers of apprentice training find they can't fill their places because they don't get enough applicants of the right calibre. Reports from the field indicate this seems to be happening a lot these days.

So what is it about today's youth? Are they no longer

interested in learning a trade? Why is it they don't queue up for apprenticeships any more?

In some circles it has always been popular to blame the schools for failing to impress youngsters with the benefits of going into industry and acquiring manual skills. But was this any different 20 or 30 years ago? Indeed, the tale of the teacher who told a pupil who couldn't do his sums properly that he'd end up doing an apprenticeship is as old as the hills.

In looking for reasons why apprenticeships may have gone out of fashion with modern youth we have to look at what may have changed in the way people leaving school view industry and jobs in industry. What's different?

First and foremost, of course, there is industry's image to consider. Let's face it, industry's image as a provider of good secure employment isn't so squeaky clean anymore. Once upon a time it was traditional for son to follow father into father's trade. Now it is more likely father will be warning son off because father has been on the receiving end of several redundancies in the last few years. Sadly there is little anyone can do about this and some firms' reputations as hirers and firers are worse than others.

The second factor in the equation is rather less obvious. A lot of apprenticeships are only open to 16/17 year olds which rather flies in the face of the fact that these days increasing numbers of young people are staying on in full-time education. This in turn introduces the rather curious situation (curious to school leavers that is) of being 'too old at eighteen'.

Is there any reason why sixth form leavers shouldn't be considered suitable for apprenticeships?

The problem here appears to be that, because craft training takes, on average, around three to four years, completers will be over 20 years old. The significant point about this is that 20 is when the full rate for the job is paid. In other words, it is regarded as unfair to have newly qualified people on the same wage as fully skilled people.

An obvious way round this difficulty is to move away from the principle of paying people full rate automatically at the age of 20. Indeed, one firm we heard about pays a single rate to apprentices irrespective of whether they are 16, 19 or 22 years old. Another approach is to base increments on attaining NVQ levels rather than birthdays.

Apart from widening their catchment to include sixth form leavers, is there anything else recruiters can do to attract takers for apprenticeships?

Because of National Curriculum requirements schools are always on the lookout for work experience places (speak to the head or the careers teacher). We come across many small firms who source all or almost all their apprentice intake from young people they have had on work experience placements. Bear in mind, though, that if you intend to use work experience to source apprentices you need:

- to plan it carefully (have youngsters doing something rather than standing watching someone else);

- some dialogue somewhere along the line, eg 'what do you want to do when you leave school?' and 'have you thought of coming to work here?'. Practitioners with experience report that this kind of dialogue can be best instigated by people on the shop floor – skilled people themselves;

- to explain to them how to apply for a job in the company;

- to re-establish contact with good ex-work experience people before they leave school (taking into account that a full year may have lapsed since the work experience placement). You could perhaps invite them to attend an open evening (eg video presentation, short speech from the MD, invitation to bring mum or dad).

Industry is in many ways its own best advocate. Without wishing to point any fingers, part of the problem with school leavers, we feel, is that they are getting most of their information second-hand – from teachers, career officers and indeed from parents. Pupils on work experience offer the unique opportunity for industry to deal direct and this opportunity should be taken.

RETENTION OF APPRENTICES

Investing money in assets which can walk off at any minute is, unfortunately, one way of looking at training. Turnover among skilled people is bad enough. Turnover among ex-apprentices you have spent years training is even worse.

In our recruitment business we see a fair share of young people who have recently completed apprenticeships and who want to put themselves on the market for the first time. Admittedly their aspirations are sometimes naïve. They are looking for jobs which aren't available or are only available to people with far more experience. When they discover the grass isn't as green on the other side of the fence as they thought it was they usually end up staying put and the firms they work for are none the wiser.

There is another category of ex-apprentice however. This is the under-recognised variety.

Take Neil. Neil is 23, a press toolmaker and still with the firm where he served his apprenticeship. Neil is paid £5.25 per hour whereas the other toolmakers are earning £6.50. Neil's boss, the toolroom manager, has told Neil he can't be put on the £6.50 rate until he proves himself capable of doing jobs on his own from start to finish. Neil regards this as unfair. He has been in the toolroom seven years now and in his opinion he can do any job which comes into the shop. The problem is he isn't given the chance. Neil now reckons his only option is to leave. If he doesn't, he'll always be treated as an apprentice.

There are a lot of Neils about. Eventually, with a bit of persistence, Neil will find a job which pays him £6.50 an hour – or more.

How many firms can put up their hands and say 'not guilty' when it comes to under-recognising home grown talent?

Here is another example.

Diddyparts is a precision engineering business producing tiny machined components which are used in the electronics industry. Diddyparts have just invested huge sums of money in a brand new, state of the art cnc machining centre with dedicated software. At first Diddyparts tried recruiting an experienced programmer/setter/operator on the outside market. This gave them a nasty shock because all the candidates they saw were looking for basic pay in excess of £17 000 a year. Diddyparts top rate for a skilled machinist is £7.20 an hour. It was at this point that the machine shop manager hit on the idea of talking to Nick. Nick is a young machinist just out of his apprenticeship. Nick is very interested in learning about cnc machining and he is attending an evening class at the local Technical college. Nick is currently on the standard machinist's rate (£6.10 an hour).

The deal the machine shop manager puts to Nick is this.

Nick is sent on a manufacturer's course to learn how to set and operate the new machine and how to programme the software. In recognition of his new skills Nick's rate will increase to £6.75 an hour.

Everyone is happy. Nick because he's got an increase and a chance he wanted (to get practical experience on cnc machining). Diddyparts because they've not having to pay him £17k. OK, so Nick may be lacking in cnc experience but at least he knows the kind of work that Diddyparts do. He knows what quality standards the customers expect.

How long it will take for Nick's euphoria to wear off is anyone's guess. Sooner or later though, particularly as he gains more experience, Nick is bound to realise that people of his calibre can earn a lot more elsewhere and he would be the exception if he didn't try putting this to the test (by shopping around). And when he lands a job at £17k plus, Diddyparts will have to decide whether to buy him off or whether to let him go and try and find another cnc programmer/setter/operator on the cheap, ie another Nick.

If Diddyparts do decide to match his offer and Nick stays then a certain amount of feelgood will have been lost. The fact that he had to put his notice in to get what he sees as a fair rate for the job will stick in Nick's craw for a long time.

Lesson: don't treat your ex-apprentices as skilled people on the cheap. It's a surefire way of losing them and putting you in the position of having to pay higher rates anyway to entice people from outside. The benefits from training are completely lost.

JUSTIFYING THE COSTS OF TRAINING

We appreciate that in directing this message to get stuck into training or give more training, in nine cases out of ten we are going to be preaching to the converted.

The brake on training expenditure is usually applied higher up the ladder and one of the major concerns of people at the sharp end of skills shortages (the people with the problems) is winning enough funding for the levels of apprentice training they need.

Training has a cost, and this can be measured with reasonable accuracy in terms of apprentice wages, fees, overheads on dedicated training areas and so on. What we frequently find, though, is that in justifying the costs of training, practitioners understate the alternative – the real cost of not training or not training in sufficient volumes.

The fact that the number crunching on these occasions is often done by management accountants doesn't help either. Management accountants will only react to information fed to them but, even if you're doing the sums yourself, what you need to check out is that you are including everything on the debit side of not training.

Here is a checklist of costs we think you need to take into account when making the comparison between training and not training; the costs in other words of having to live with skills shortages on an ongoing basis.

- The opportunity cost: the cost of not being able to take on work or provide an adequate service to customers.

- Alternatively, perhaps, the cost of having to put remaining skilled people on overtime or having to put work out, eg to providers of sub-contract services.

- The cost of employing temps (if you can get them).

- Sourcing costs – advertising or fees you have to pay to recruitment consultants.

- The time you have to devote to skilled recruitment. There is an opportunity cost here too. If you're dedicating time to skilled recruitment it prevents you doing anything else.

- Add-on costs if you have to recruit out of area.

- The premium you have to pay to entice people to join you – the knock-on effect this is going to have on your existing rates. Don't think you are going to get away with things here. Exposure to competitive markets (markets for scarce people) exacts a big price.

To make these figures real you have to build in an estimate of the attrition rate of your skilled workforce – the labour turnover. You can draw on historical experience here, but remember not to base historical experience on recessionary periods when turnover will have been low.

SUMMARY

If you don't train sufficiently you will pay the price. Firms who provide skills training (apprenticeships) are quids in.

16

Questions and Answers

REASONS FOR SKILLS SHORTAGES

People who have quit their trades

Question

What about people who have left skilled employment involuntarily, eg redundancy casualties from several years ago who took whatever happened to be going at the time? Can't we coax some of these people back?

Answer

One of the big difficulties here is that in our experience employers show a decided reluctance to take on people who have been out of their trades for a number of years. The fear we hear voiced is such people will have 'lost touch' – a reflection perhaps of the onward march of technology or perhaps just a way of articulating the general unwillingness these days to take risks with people.

SEEKING REASONS FOR RETENTION DIFFICULTIES

Leavers' Questionnaires

Question

Because of the pressure on management time we could not contemplate carrying out systematic termination interviews. What we thought of doing though was giving each leaver a questionnaire to fill in. What do you think?

Answer

A lot depends on the questions. For instance if you ask 'why are you leaving?' then give a number of boxes to tick ranging from 'more money' to 'any other reason' we feel you probably won't learn a lot. On the other hand, more probing questions (such as questions on future employment and earnings) run the risk of not being answered or not being answered fully. On the whole open-ended questions would probably be best. Try your questionnaires by all means but don't be too disappointed if they don't give you the kind of feedback you are looking for. Use them for a trial period perhaps.

Termination interviews carried out by consultants

Question

With a view to saving management time and to try to get some professionalism and objectivity into our termination interviews we are contemplating using consultants to do them for us. Are there any snags?

Answer

Yes, it's going to be expensive. Bear in mind people don't leave in nice tidy batches either so we can envisage your consultants having to 'to and fro' a lot, with you doubtless footing the bill for their travelling time. Cheaper than a consultant you might find a retired personnel manager happy to provide you with the same kind of service on a 'pop in when needed' basis. Maybe the local branch of the Institute of Personnel & Development could put you in touch with someone?

STOPPING SKILLED PEOPLE LEAVING: RETENTION DEVICES

Restraint Clauses – People Won't Sign Them

Question

Our experience with restraint clauses – even with middle management – is that people won't sign them. So what's the use of putting them to people on the shop floor?

Answer

We agree, you're probably wasting your time unless you happen to be offering some big package of which restraints are a part. Restraints, we repeat, are not for general usage at this level.

People take no notice of restraints

Question

It's a well-known fact that employers don't bother enforcing restraints. So won't people just sign on the dotted line, take what's on offer, then put their two fingers up when they leave?

Answer

Possibly. The force of restraints, however, is not on the person who is bound by it but on the firm who is contemplating employing that person. It's a deterrent – no more, no less.

Employees working extended notice – not always what you want

Question

We employ a large number of skilled people and, while we would be more than happy to have the majority working out a month's notice there is a fringe element who we know we would have problems with. As we see it differentiating between people (being selective as to who we put on a month's notice) is inviting all sorts of trouble. Is there any alternative?

Answer

With the people you see as potentially troublesome you could always cut their extended notice period short and pay them off in lieu. Check your conditions of employment and see if you have given yourself the facility to do this. If not it might be worth inserting a clause at the same time as you extend notice periods.

Recontacting leavers – who should do it?

Question

Have you any advice on who would be the best person to make contact with people who have left? For example, should it be the line manager or someone from the human resources department?

Answer

If it is down to a choice we would pick the line manager every time because, for the trick to work, leavers have to feel certain the boss wants them back. Presenting the human resources officer as a kind of front may take some of the credibility away from what you are trying to do.

Getting a third party to contact leavers

Question

What about getting someone from outside the company to act as an intermediary (honest broker) in opening up negotiations with people who have left?

Answer

We're not sure who you have in mind but the answer is much the same as the answer to the last question. Also, try not to see this as a negotiation (a case where an honest broker *may* help). The object to phoning up ex-employees is to see if all's well and, if not, to lay the way open for them to come back. In our view this is best said straight by someone who counts – not by a mystery voice whose status is uncertain to the ex-employee.

Recontacting leavers contrary to company policy

Question

We have a rule that we do not re-employ people who leave. We think our rule is a good rule because it makes people think twice about putting their notice in. They know without asking there is no way back. Contacting employees after they have left, in our view, sends out completely the opposite signal. People will feel they have nothing to lose from going and chancing their arm on the outside job market. Suffice to say we believe our approach works and we point to the fact that our labour turnover in skilled areas is extremely low. We don't see any reason for changing what we are doing. Do you?

Answer

No. Whatever works for you, stick with it. But more to the point, if you don't have retention problems then there's no reason why you should be looking at retention devices, is there?

ARE YOU PAYING ENOUGH?

New firm in town paying very high rates

Question

A big multinational manufacturing company has recently opened a new factory in our area. To recruit the labour they need – particularly the skilled labour – they have been offering very high rates – rates which we and other local firms can't possibly afford to pay. We have already lost a dozen or so people we can ill afford to lose. Given that we can't match the money is there anything else we can do?

Answer

Very often the only salvation in these situations is that the newcomer will eventually fill all its vacancies and at that point the rot stops. Is there anything you can do? Try our suggestion of contacting leavers a few months after they have gone. These glitter jobs with big money often have hidden snags – and new factories are prone to all sorts of unforeseen problems. It's worth a go.

Top payer can't recruit

Question

Without a doubt we pay the top rates in our trade and area for the skills we employ yet still we can't recruit. What's our problem?

Answer

One of two we suspect. *Either* your methods are wrong *or* you are facing genuine scarcity and hence paying top rates won't necessarily help. Accessibility is frequently at the root of problems which companies like yours have. You pay good rates but outside your immediate circle no-one knows about it. Stating rates of pay (eg in ads or on cards in Job Centres) is one way of addressing lack of pay accessibility. If you don't like this idea then make sure your applicants know about your good rates as early on in the recruitment process as possible – for example in your very first telephone contact.

Reluctant to pay top rates to starters

Question

We employ a large number of skilled people. While our top rates (the rates we pay to our key long-serving employees) are very good, the rates we start new people on are rather less attractive. We take the view that people have to prove themselves before they get on the top rate. As you have probably guessed, we have few retention problems but recruitment is always difficult for us. Any suggestions?

Answer

This may again be an accessibility issue – making applicants aware (telling them early on in the recruitment process) that they can, in time, aspire to much higher rates. Some idea of how long will of course help – and here it may be worth formalising the way in which you move people up through pay grades, ie three months on this rate, three months on the next rate and so on. This kind of certainty about pay progression will help destroy any feeling that what you are holding back in terms of eventual earnings is pie in the sky. Give them the message: *it's real, it's attainable and it's attainable in x period of time.* Also, golden hellos may help you but it would be better by far if you didn't have to use them. Golden hellos, remember, come under desperate measures which you don't move on to until you've got your basic recruitment methods right.

Not paying skilled people for overtime

Question

About five years ago the firm put through a staff status deal for skilled grades which included such conditions as not clocking in and full pay during sickness absence for up to six months. One of the features of this deal was no payment for overtime and, instead, people were put on annualised salaries equating to previous earnings for 48 hours (40 hours basic plus 8 hours overtime which is about the average in our plant). When we're recruiting our salaries sound extremely good so we find ourselves having to emphasise to applicants that there's no extra pay if they have to work overtime and that they will be required to work overtime as and when required. Inevitably this leads to questions about how much overtime and here we have to tell them it depends on production and maintenance requirements which vary enormously, as you would expect. We find applicants think we're being evasive with them and we're sure this is why we get a lot of fall out during our selection process. We're sure people feel they might be committing themselves to a long hours job which when calculated back to an hourly rate, would show a very poor figure. In other words we're being viewed as poor payers which isn't really true. Is there any way round this problem?

Answer

Deal in facts. Get out the actual average overtime worked by people in your skilled grades over, say, a year, then work this back into an hourly rate. In other words, you do the calculation for them. Say 'the annual salary is so and so, the average number of hours overtime is so and so and if you were on a hourly rate (which you won't be of course) this would equate to £x an hour'. What you are doing here is making your pay arrangements accessible to people who think in terms of being paid by the hour. Another point here is that some skilled people prefer being salaried because it gives them stable earnings patterns. If your ads are accessible therefore – if the fact that you pay straight salaries comes across – then these are the people you will be encouraging to apply. These are the people too who won't be giving you retention problems if you go through periods when demand for overtime working is high.

UNDERSTANDING SKILLED PEOPLE

Psychometric tests – do they put candidates off?

Question

In your case study (Chris, see page 26) you mentioned psychometric tests and candidates having no idea what they are. We give all our applicants psychometric tests and we wonder perhaps whether we ought to be putting an explanatory note in with our letters inviting people to interview. What do you think? On the other hand, do you think our psychometric tests might be putting skilled candidates off? Might we be better dropping them altogether?

Answer

We have no evidence of psychometric tests actually putting candidates off. On the contrary, we find most of our skilled people enjoy doing them – and are keen to know the result. Our only quarrel with psychometric tests and tests in general is where they are allowed to slow selection procedures up and thereby encourage candidate fall out. Your explanatory note sounds a good idea by the way.

Breakfast interviews

Question

I'm an early morning person so if I have to do interviews out of hours I would much prefer to do these first thing. Is this going to cause me any problems?

Answer

It really depends on your applicants. Some may be early risers like you; others may find the prospect of a 6am grilling too much of an ordeal to contemplate. If you get voice contact with your candidates – which you will do if you run a telephone hotline for example – then you will be able to gauge who is happy to come first thing in the morning (before work) and who isn't. Be careful though that you don't unintentionally superimpose your own preferences here, eg 'I can see you at 6am on Thursday – is that OK?'. Candidates will find it hard to say no without giving you the impression they can't get out of bed in the morning. Best, we would say, to offer candidates a choice of before work or after work or on Saturday morning. Sorry we can't keep you clear of late nights at the office but better for you by far if your candidates turn up.

Candidates who shop round

Question

My experience of skilled people is there are a lot of them who are just permanently shopping round for the best money they can get. Making yourself accessible, available and everything else you suggest is, in my book, playing right into their hands. What do you say to that?

Answer

There are people who shop round but we would disagree with you on the numbers. We would say they are a small minority and more prevalent in some trades than others (eg toolmakers or people in those kinds of trades which, for traditional reasons, concentrate on small geographical areas). We say this because a lot of this shopping round is in the form of door knocking – people who do the rounds calling in to see if there are any vacancies. Sometimes they take an afternoon off work for the purpose.

Coming back to the point you have raised, our worry for you is that by shutting the door on people you view as nuisances you will be shutting the door on everyone. Availability is about getting the door open, wide, and yes, this means you are going to be exposing yourself to timewasters – not just people who are shopping round but people whose skills you are going to view as unsatisfactory too. We are encouraging you, if you like, to take a few risks with timewasters – for the greater good of being able to recruit the people you need.

Offering the facility to change interview appointments

Question

Will it help if I actually tell people I have listed for interview to ring in if the time and date are inconvenient? Taking your availability point, would it help further if I gave them my home phone number where I can be contacted in the evening?

Answer

You will remember we gave you three reasons why people don't ring in if interview times are difficult:

- They prejudge the response. They think if they ask for out of hours appointments the answer will be no.

- They find it difficult to make phone calls in normal office hours.

- They feel they're being awkward.

Giving your home phone number disposes of the problem of making calls from work. Saying they can rearrange and telling them how to do it goes some way towards removing any feeling of being awkward or that the barriers will automatically go up if they suggest an appointment out of hours. We still stick to the view, however, that the best way to set up interviews is by talking it through – which you can do, for example, if you set up a phone-in line.

Doing evening interviews only

Question

Surely one way to avoid availability difficulties is by setting aside an evening for interviews and giving candidates times to come along? From our point of view, it saves having to talk to them beforehand and we do the interviews in one straight session. Is there anything wrong with this?

Answer

Some of your candidates may be shiftworkers (you won't know). Some may be committed to overtime on the evening you choose or alternatively they may have social/domestic commitments. Then you are putting your candidates in the position of having to rearrange, with all the associated problems.

Pay accessibility problem – no fixed pay scales

Question

We're a small company and we don't have fixed pay scales. We prefer to negotiate rates of pay on an individual basis. With new starters the rate of pay tends to reflect skills, experience and what the candidate is looking for. We like this kind of flexibility and we feel it helps us to recruit the right people. Our difficulty, of course, is that we can't put a rate of pay in an ad and we are reluctant to put a range because applicants are inclined to focus on the higher figure. Any suggestions?

Answer

The point about pay accessibility is that pre-interview both you and the candidate know you're not wasting one another's time. Suggestions? If you do a phone-in you can ask candidates to tell you what they're looking for. If the figure is way over the top you can say so. If it's within the range you pay then a comment like 'that's OK providing your experience and skills match up to what we're looking for', will suffice – and move straight on to setting up the interview.

Pay accessibility – we pay poor rates

Question

We have no objection in principle to putting our rates of pay in the paper but we don't because we know they're poor and they will only serve to put candidates off. We've always felt our best bet is to try at least to get people to come in for an interview in the hope we might be able to establish some common ground with them. In our situation what else can we do?

Answer

Could it be you're suffering from pay paranoia? Remember what we said about the number of firms who convince themselves they're at the bottom of the pay heap when in fact they're a long way off it. Try putting your rates in an ad (a good ad with maximum availability and accessibility) and see what success you have. You may be pleasantly surprised. Alternatively, if the response is poor, you will have moved a step closer to proving whether your problems are because of pay or because of genuine scarcity. Go through the checklist on page 73 too. This will eliminate the x factors which can creep into reasons for poor response to ads.

SOURCES OF SKILLED PEOPLE

Vacancies Boards

Question

Years ago we used to have a vacancies board outside the factory gate which disappeared in one of our many reorganisations. With all this emphasis you are putting on accessibility, could there be a place for bringing the vacancies board back in some modified form?

Answer

Firms with premises adjacent to busy main roads used to attach great importance to vacancies boards. We don't claim to have made any great study into why so many of them went but we would hazard a guess that they became an acute embarrassment in lean periods such as the early 80s recession. Bringing back vacancies boards is certainly an interesting idea and, let's face it, there aren't many options available in recruitment which come completely free as vacancies boards do. The advent of electronic noticeboards of various descriptions also opens up all sorts of possibilities (eg full information on jobs rather than just job titles together with detailed information on how to apply etc).

Encouraging employee introductions

Question

We are suffering from acute skills shortages and we are considering a cash incentive scheme to encourage employees to introduce people they know – skilled people, that is. Our recruitment problems are now so we want to encourage employees to act straight away. Any suggestion as to how we can do this?

Answer

Make the payments attractive (certainly not less than £100) and put the scheme in for a fixed period – say three months. This will encourage employees to hurry up with their introductions. It will also prevent you from being saddled with the scheme when you no longer have any vacancies (which is an awkward situation). The scheme can always be resurrected or extended.

Employee Introduction Schemes – argument over qualifying rules

Question

We put in an employee introduction scheme last year for the kind of people we were having problems recruiting ie skilled production workers. The difficulty is that employees have been introducing people who aren't really skilled and we have had endless arguments with individuals who feel they are entitled to payments. In some cases – and in hindsight wrongly – we have given way just to keep the peace. We can't honestly say we have managed to recruit a single skilled person yet. Is there anything we should be doing with our scheme?

Answer

Yes – drop it. Your time is precious and it's no good at all if you are spending it settling petty quarrels and achieving nothing.

Sources – Job Centres sending the wrong people

Question

We've tried recruiting skilled people from the Job Centre and we're getting fed up. Every time they send us people who are completely unsuitable. What can we do about this?

Answer

Speak to the manager but – and this is a big but – remember that candidates from Job Centres are self selecting. Any Tom, Dick or Sheila can read the cards on display and ask to have their name put forward. It's up to you to do the sifting out.

Asking Job Centres to get candidates to fill in application forms

Question

We have had a lot of problems in the past with the local Job Centre sending down time wasters for skilled jobs. Someone suggested we gave the Job Centre a stock of our standard application forms so anyone who enquired about one of our skilled vacancies would have to fill a form in first and send to us. Is this a good idea?

Answer

Genuine skilled people might be put off. A better idea in our view would be to ask the Job Centre staff to give enquirers your phone number – or put it on the card they display. A quick chat over the phone will enable you to establish whether the candidate is skilled or not. If you are satisfied you are speaking to someone *bona fide* you can move on quickly to setting up an interview. Incidentally, notifying vacancies to Job Centres can be run in with phone-in lines and open sessions. The information on the card will simply tell candidates to ring in or call in at the times you want them to, ie you are using your Job Centre sourcing in parallel with advertising.

Consultants will do a better job than we can

Question

We have had many problems recruiting skilled people. We are contemplating bringing in consultants to do an exercise for us start to finish. Is there anything we need to be looking out for?

Answer

What you are contemplating saddens us in many ways because you will make a far better job of recruiting than any consultant if you follow the lessons in this book. At best all consultants can do for you is save you your time (at a cost of course). At worst they can botch the whole thing by not applying the principles we have called the 3As. Please think again.

Advertising: giving closing dates

Question

It has always been a practice in this company to put closing dates for applications in our advertisements. Is this a good idea?

Answer

On the one hand a closing date impresses a sense of urgency on applicants. On the other you could be shutting the door on people who, for example, have been away on holiday or out of town on a job. On balance we would probably say no to closing dates. If your methods of application include phone-ins or open houses, when to apply becomes self defining of course.

Two insertion dates for advertisements

Question

When we place recruitment advertising material we always ask for two insertions. We have had to ask questions about this recently because of the cost. In your opinion what would we be losing if we went down to one insertion only?

Answer

In our opinion not a lot – and frankly we are always surprised at the number of companies who place advertisements in newspapers two nights running. For a start, we find newspapers are not very charitable when it comes to offering discounts so two insertions usually means double the cost. Secondly, if one ad appears on the jobs night (Thursday) then the chances are ad number two will appear on Friday neatly tucked in among the second hand car ads. Thirdly, and in our view most importantly, there is this over-exposure problem – 'it's them again, why are they always advertising?'. In the long run it puts candidates off.

Job Night is on Friday

Question

In our local rag job night is on Friday night which is a pain. Should we stick to job night or should we put our ads in on a night earlier in the week? If we do stick to Friday then how do we slot in two open sessions or phone-ins? Please don't have us working on Saturday.

Answer

Yes it is a pain but do stick to job night (Friday). Open sessions and phone-ins? You could run them on Friday and Monday. This would also give a facility to people who read the ads over the weekend.

USING ADVERTISING MORE EFFECTIVELY

Methods of application: CVs

Question

What about CVs? Are you saying that asking skilled candidates to submit a CV isn't a good idea?

Answer

What we are most definitely saying is that one single method of applying – CVs or anything else – isn't a good idea and that giving candidates alternatives will enhance the response. Suggest candidates send a CV by all means but make sure there is an alternative for them so you won't be shutting the doors on someone who hasn't got a CV or who will need to update their CV.

More than one vacancy

Question

In a few weeks' time we will have a number of vacancies for sheet metal workers because we are opening up a new fabrication department. The general manager is concerned that if we advertise for sheet metal workers (plural) it might give the impression people are leaving – which isn't true. Do you have a view on this?

Answer

There are two opposing schools of thought on advertising plurals:

- it is bad for the reason your general manager has expressed;
- it is good because it encourages more people to apply because they will feel there is more chance of getting the job.

One way round the problem is to advertise in the plural but to make it clear in the copy that the jobs are new jobs – additionals rather than replacements for leavers.

Timing of ads

Question

We are planning the expansion of a new factory in several phases. At each phase there will be an intake of approximately 20 personnel of which around five will be skilled. The skilled people are essential and at the start of one of these phases we would not want to find ourselves short of skilled people. Because of the problems we have had up to now in recruiting skilled people this seems to indicate to us that we must give ourselves plenty of time. What bothers me though is that we could start recruiting too soon and fall into the trap of losing some people because of the length of time between offering them the job and the actual starting date. In short we would be no better off. Can you help me solve my dilemma?

Answer

You are very wise to anticipate this problem. We have come across numerous firms who have had to put expansion plans on hold simply because they haven't been able to recruit skilled people in time for a start-up date. Bearing in mind we are not living in a perfect world, one way out of your difficulty would be to start the skilled recruiting early and bring suitable people on board as soon as you find them, even if this means some of them will be joining you before your phase start date. This is a question of balancing the risks: which cost is biggest – paying out a few weeks' extra wages to people who may be kicking their heels or having to put your expansion programme back indefinitely? The answer seems obvious.

Choice of media – trade journals

Question

A lot of our engineers pick up the trade journal which circulates in our industry. We even occasionally catch them flicking through the job ads. We have never used a trade journal for advertising skilled vacancies. Could we be missing out?

Answer

Trade journals, with few exceptions, are national publications which means the response to ads in them can come from anywhere. Bearing in mind you are not onto desperate measures yet, relocating people from other parts of the country may not be an expense or a risk you want at this stage. Hopefully you will of course get some response to an ad in a trade journal from your own area but, because the readership of these trade journals is restricted, this response won't, on average, be as good as the response you can get from the local evening paper on job night. Certainly don't, therefore, use the trade journal as an *alternative* to the local evening paper. If you do use it, treat it as an add-on. Trade journals can be useful in some situations – if, for example, you are recruiting a national field service team with vacancies in all areas.

Guaranteeing interviews

Question

We thought of putting in our ads that anyone who applies is guaranteed an interview. Is it not the case that many people are put off applying for jobs because they don't get interviews? Will our idea therefore get us a better response?

Answer

One of the reasons why open sessions are such powerful recruiting tools is because they enable applicants to come face to face with employers without having to go through what they see as a lot of preliminaries. Phone-ins have the same appeal except they're voice to voice. Your thinking is therefore along the right lines but as we see it, there is no need to guarantee interviews if you're running open sessions and phone-ins. Open sessions and phone-ins have other benefits for you too.

Not wanting to hear from previous applicants

Question

At various points you have been pretty scathing about firms who put 'no previous applicants' in their ads. I can appreciate how it automatically flags up that the position's been open for some time but how do you discourage previous applicants otherwise?

Answer

The short answer is you don't. You put up with them because this is about opening doors for applicants, not shutting them out. The risk, as we see it, is in any event minimal. Take an open session. If a previous applicant decides to turn up there is nothing you can do about it. On the other hand all you're committed to is a five minute chat which might end with 'here is an application form – fill it in and let us have it back' (no mention of interviews).

Late applicants: people who miss open sessions and phone-ins

Question

What about late applicants? We have in mind the kind of people who put the job ads to one side and read them on Sunday or people who hear about jobs from friends. They will have missed the phone-ins or open session so won't we in effect be excluding them?

Answer

Hold on, who said anything about phone-ins and open sessions being the *only* method of applying? Remember what we told you about always offering people choices. If in addition to your phone-ins and open sessions you also have the facility for applicants to write in or send a CV then the latecomers won't be excluded.

Pay accessibility using box numbers and confidential reply advertisements

Question

We are one of those companies who don't like putting our rates of pay in ads. Can you comment please on using box numbers and confidential reply services as an alternative?

Answer

Box numbers are a bit of a turn off, more so today because of this general feeling of wariness with which a lot of people approach the job market. Confidential reply, with the facility to give a list of firms you don't want your application sent to, is a slight advance but on the whole you would be best over-coming pay inaccessibility in the way we suggest, ie set up a phone-in and make the rate of pay one of the first subjects you discuss with applicants.

CONVERTING APPLICANTS INTO STARTERS

Preliminary and second interviews

Question (from an HR practitioner)

One of the reasons we have preliminary interviews is so that we can sift out any unsuitable candidates before line managers see them. If we do preliminary and final interviews end-on as you suggest we won't be able to do this. Isn't this inviting criticism from line managers who will feel we're not doing our jobs properly?

Answer

You can still sift out. You won't be sending any unsuitable candidates along for your line manager to see, will you? In these situations you need to explain to line managers that some candidates will be coming to see them and some won't – and the reason why. Hopefully managers will be appreciative to see you've got some candidates for them at last.

Phoning candidates up to find out why they didn't attend their interviews

Question

Is there any mileage in phoning up candidates who don't attend interviews to see what the reason is?

Answer

We would like to say yes but in practice we have to admit our experience has been pretty negative. The typical response is an embarrassed silence followed by a limp excuse or 'I forgot' or, if they're honest, a list of reasons why they'd had second thoughts about the job. If we're looking at ways and means of putting your time to profitable use then phoning up non-attenders isn't one of them. Bear in mind too that nine times out of ten you won't be able to get most of these people till after 6.00pm.

RESOURCES

Paying HR staff for overtime

Question

Our HR staff aren't normally paid for overtime but we took the view that the two open sessions and phone-ins we ran to fill some skilled vacancies were extraordinary. Hence we paid the staff for the overtime they put in on a one-off basis. Presumably you would see no problem with this?

Answer

Not if you do it every time.

Running phone-ins and open sessions at the same time

Question

Can we do our phone-ins and open sessions on the same evenings? Apart from keeping the late nights to a minimum we would be reducing the time we take for sourcing, ie part of compressing our selection procedures.

Answer

The more people you have on duty the easier it becomes to run phone-ins and open sessions at the same time. Be warned though, it can get chaotic! Firms where recruitment is down to one person would not really be advised to try this. In such circumstances it might be best to have the phone-in on the night the ad appears and the open session the following day.

Using freephones

Question

Would it get us better response if we used a freephone number for our hotline?

Answer

We can claim no experience with freephone numbers but when the subject comes up for discussion, as it does from time to time, most recruiters seem to feel they might act as off putters.

Answering machines

Question

You have totally dismissed telephone answering machines. We appreciate some callers won't leave a message but won't they be just a minority? Losing a few applicants seems a small price to pay for avoiding sitting in the office half the night.

Answer

Please remember, phone-ins have a wider purpose. You need to talk to the applicants, firstly to form a broad assessment of their suitability and secondly to find out when they can attend interviews. We think you will gain in response terms too if you can put 'no answering machines' next to your hotline number in your ad.

Mobile phones

Question

Can you divert a line with Star Services onto a mobile phone?

Answer

Yes you can but we are not recommending you try it. Apart from the cost to the unsuspecting caller, mobile phone reception is too variable in quality for these purposes.

One woman Human Resources Department

Question

The Human Resources department in this company consists of one overworked female, namely me! I take in everything you have to say about recruiting skilled people but in my case your suggestions would give me two problems:

1. *If I did phone-ins and open sessions I would have to do them without any assistance.*

2. *I would be left on my own in the office at night (we are in an inner city area).*

Can you offer me any advice?

Answer

Your safety is paramount. If you can't get help with after-hours open sessions then don't do them. By their very nature they have to be 'open to the street'. Furthermore, introducing access restrictions will reduce their effectiveness anyway. Phone-ins are a different matter because you can do them at home or anywhere else you choose.

Star Services – knowing if a call diversion is in operation

Question

Using Star Services, is there any way of knowing if a call diversion is in operation? In other words, when I come into the office in the morning how can I check to make sure that the diversion signal has been cancelled?

Answer

This is easy. The dialling tone has a pause every few seconds. If you hear this it means your line is still diverted.

Are Star Services difficult to use?

Question

I'm a complete illiterate when it comes to using new technology. Are these Star Services difficult to learn to operate?

Answer

Star Services have a number of facilities of which you will be using just two. To divert your incoming calls to another number all you have to do is press * 21 * followed by the number you want your calls to go to followed by #. Undiverting is even easier (# 21 #). Putting a divert on busy signal on to your line is a similar very simple procedure.

Combining interviews with open sessions

Question

Taking your point about compressing procedures to reduce candidate fall out, why not go a step further and combine open days with selection interviews? We appreciate this means interviewing people as they step in off the street but if there aren't going to be that many of them we don't see where the problem arises.

Answer

Open sessions, like phone-ins, are powerful sourcing tools and we frequently get firms who have previously advertised with little success finding themselves overwhelmed with responses when they try them for the first time. When you run an open session you literally have no idea what's going to happen and if you have planned to extend the recommended five minute chats into full-blown interviews with line managers standing by ready to see the 'suitables', then you might find yourself rapidly getting into a mess if large numbers of applicants decide to turn up. You have no control over who walks through the door and this is the difficult bit. With experience behind you, however, you can start to become more adventurous. For instance, you will get to know what kind of turnouts are normal for your area and for the trades you are trying to recruit. You might well be able to consider combining sourcing and interviewing. Flexibility is important too. With very scarce skills, if the ideal candidate (ie the kind of person you've been trying to recruit for the last six months) just happens to walk through the door then you will be falling over yourself to bend the procedures, won't you?

Open sessions as major events

Question

We have used open days and open evenings for recruitment with great success and over many years. These are on a much grander scale than the kind of open sessions you describe with factory tours, exhibitions of products, showings of a specially commissioned 20 minute company recruitment film and a buffet laid on. People who want to apply for jobs can be interviewed there and then – and we have HR staff and managers on standby. The kind of open sessions you describe are presumably intended for smaller firms with limited resources. Is this so?

Answer

They are intended for anyone but big recruitment events like you have in mind and dedicated skills sourcing open sessions of the type we describe are really two entirely different animals. Big events, providing they run on after hours, can and do work for skills recruiters, as you have found, because they can claim all-important availability. This is despite the fact that they are frequently open to all comers, ie skilled and other vacancies are mixed (which, as we have said in text, will tend to depress skilled response). The difficulty with big events, though, is that you won't want to stage one just to fill one skilled vacancy and sadly this is why a lot of firms revert to classic inaccessible and unavailable forms of recruiting. In short, even big event holders like you may still have a use for our kind of sessions with their one- and two-off vacancies.

DESPERATE MEASURES

Advertising in other areas – using national tabloids

Question

We have been living with skills shortages for many months. Our history, briefly, is that we relocated into a rural area over 20 years ago but our skills training has never kept up with our growth. The area, however, has many attractions and we are now looking at the possibility of relocating skilled people from other parts of the country. One of my colleagues has suggested we advertise in a national tabloid. Is this something you can recommend?

Answer

No, for two reasons:

- Buy a few tabloids and have a look. National tabloids tend to contain a curious mix of recruitment advertising. As one of our candidates put it – not too kindly – 'that's where you get all the Mickey Mouse jobs!' Not all jobs in national tabloids are Mickey Mouse jobs, we hasten to add, but as sources of skilled people (and we speak as we find) local evening papers on jobs nights are far more effective.

- You will have problems handling the response. Applications will come from here, there and everywhere which – unless you can fit in a whistle-stop tour of the country – prevents you from doing your preliminary interviewing locally. This, as we have seen, will be a cause of candidate fall out. This difficulty doesn't of course apply just to tabloids.

I can only recruit people on temp to perm

Question

We have a recruiting problem with skilled people and we are well aware of the reason why. We are part of a group and one of the edicts we have had from group head office is that we can only employ people on a temp to perm basis. The temp period in question is twelve weeks. We have tried reassuring candidates that our temp to perm is as good as a proper offer of employment but on the whole they don't buy it. Is there anything we can do?

Answer

No – apart from convincing your head office their policy is preventing you recruiting people you badly need. Skilled people, as you have doubtless gathered, are not normally unemployed and you can't expect anyone to give up a permanent job for a temporary one. That's asking far too much.

Golden hellos not to our liking

Question

We have taken on board all you have to say about making our ads more accessible and offering phone-ins and open sessions but we find your golden hellos hard to swallow. Frankly there would be ructions in this company if we started making big up-front payments to new people. When you suggest we should be doing this are you being totally serious?

Answer

Stop – you've misunderstood! Golden hellos come under desperate measures and under no circumstances should you be even contemplating using them until you have exhausted every other possibility. Even then you may still feel they're not for you. Certainly don't look at golden hellos or anything else in the desperate measures basket until you have put the 3As into practice using conventional methods of recruitment.

Golden hellos – are they taxable?

Question

Are these golden hellos subject to tax and NI deductions?

Answer

Yes.

Recruiting in depressed areas – using pay enticement

Question

Surely one of the facts about depressed areas is that levels of pay aren't very good? As we see it, therefore, money needs to play a major part in persuading people to leave depressed areas. Shouldn't recruiters be majoring on money?

Answer

We're all for pay accessibility so we have no argument with what you are saying. Don't imagine though that money is the magic pull force which will overcome all. If the ties to a depressed area are strong (ie the push forces are weak) people are still going to take a lot of shifting.

Selecting target areas – doing research

Question

Before targeting an area for recruitment would it not be sensible to carry out some research into the kinds of people who are available?

Answer

The kind of time scales skills recruiters have to work to usually preclude research in the sense you mean. In any event, perhaps an ad in the local evening paper will tell you more about labour conditions than anything you could find in published research.

Relocation costs – are we paying enough?

Question

Our relocation package hasn't changed for many years. With single people we offer to pay bed and breakfast accommodation for six weeks. With families, we meet removal expenses and the usual costs associated with buying and selling houses plus a modest curtains and carpets allowance. Do you think this is adequate? We don't really get involved in relocation that often so we are possibly out of touch with trends.

Answer

Your relocation package probably isn't that untypical for people outside senior jobs. If we would encourage you to do anything it would be to deal with relocation flexibly taking individual circumstances into account.

Seeking to claw back relocation expenses

Question

We are in an area where skilled jobs are plentiful and competition for skilled people is intense. We have been looking at recruiting in other parts of the country but we can see a situation where we relocate someone from one of these job blackspots then find, as soon as we've footed the bills, the person will decide to move on. Is there anything we can do to prevent people from using us in this way?

Answer

You can insert a claw back clause in your relocation contract saying the money is repayable if someone leaves within (say) twelve months. We won't pretend, however, that this is going to help you a lot beyond perhaps making people think twice. Sorry to say it but perhaps you just have to view this as one of the risks of relocating people and why you need to view recruiting out of area as a desperate measure.

ALTERNATIVE SOLUTIONS TO SKILLS SHORTAGES

Weekend shift hours not suitable to most moonlighters

Question

We have a weekend shift which consists of two twelve-hour shifts on Saturday and Sunday – days and nights rotating. This means that every fortnight our weekenders finish at 6.00am on Monday morning. We're so desperate for skilled labour we couldn't give a toss how many jobs people have got but our Monday morning finishing time does tend to rule out the weekend shift for people in normal 39 hour Monday to Friday occupations. We don't therefore have much scope for moonlighters, do we?

Answer

Is it strictly necessary you rotate your shifts? If not, your Saturday and Sunday day shifts would be perfectly OK for moonlighters. Again, this is part and parcel of adapting working hours to the people who are available.

TROUBLE SHOOTING

Wide range of skills necessary

Question

Yes, we may well be guilty of overspecifying but it doesn't get round the fact that in our engineering situations we need people who can perform an extremely wide range of tasks. What are we supposed to do? Give up?

Answer

Certainly not, but what you need to ask yourself is whether any of the people you are presently turning down could acquire the skills you need, given a reasonable amount of training. What we don't want you to do is to keep going back to fruitless recruiting exercises time and time again.

Moonlighters and the black economy

Question

Your suggestion about using moonlighters worries us. Isn't this just going to draw us into a shady world of illegal cash payments and people using false names?

Answer

Firstly a reminder that you will only be looking at moonlighters (a) if you're desperate (you've tried everything else) and (b) as a stop gap. Second job people – perhaps it's best we refer to them as that – fall into two definite types. Yes, there are those who are looking for cash in hand jobs and for employers who will pay wages without making PAYE deductions. These people, as we know, are often on benefits and claiming illegally. Clearly you should have no truck with this first type. The other type, those who have started to present themselves in increasing numbers in recent years, are people who, by and large, would shy away from doing anything illegal. Their only aspiration is to use their spare time and their skills to make more money for themselves and their families. Where have these people come from all of a sudden? Many of them, as we have said, are driven by money reasons. But coupled with this we have seen in the last 10 to 15 years the emergence of patterns of working which make second jobs possible where they weren't before. Weekend shifts are one example – continental shifts with three, four and five off days are another. Don't form the view that all second job people are shady characters with their feet in the black economy because this would be wrong. Being broke these days is perfectly respectable.

How to recruit moonlighters

Question

We've got no objection to using moonlighters but how do we go about finding them?

Answer

That's easy. You don't have to do anything special. Providing your jobs are accessible and it's plain (eg in your ads) what the working hours are then anyone with second job aspirations will present themselves automatically. What you must do, though, is to make sure that people dealing with sourcing at your end are singing from the same hymn sheet as you. We say this because we came across a company a few years ago where the personnel officer was turning away skilled second job people applying for work on a weekend shift because she felt they were unsuitable.

Moonlighters – health and safety considerations

Question

We are a responsible employer with firm views on workplace health and safety. We feel you rather gloss over the health and safety risks associated with second job people – people who will, by definition, be working large numbers of hours every week, often without rest days. Can you deal with this point please?

Answer

No-one is pretending any of these situations are ideal and we come back to the point that moonlighters, retirees and everything else we have talked about under desperate measures are ways of getting you out of a self-imposed jam, largely because you haven't trained skilled people in sufficient numbers – and let's not gloss over this either. Perhaps before any of us start getting too pious about health and safety and people who work too many hours, it may pay to reflect on how many firms bother to check out what their existing Monday to Friday employees do with their weekends.

Human resources people don't understand skilled jobs

Question

You have highlighted the problem of people in personnel departments not understanding what skilled jobs entail. Is this a case of where recruiting would be best carried out by line managers or technical people?

Answer

This has happened in some firms. Skilled recruitment has been handed over to line managers or technical people but there is a downside and the downside is that line managers and technical people often make the worst recruiters. This comment is not intended as a slight on anyone but a reflection of the fact that people with other functions to discharge won't be able to give recruitment the application it needs – they will find it much harder. If you feel your personnel department doesn't understand skilled jobs then the answer is to work on it with them.

EMPLOYMENT PACKAGES FOR SKILLED PEOPLE

Probationary periods are necessary

Question

We would be very reluctant to drop trial periods. In skilled employment we don't know whether the people we select can do the job or not – until they've been with us for several weeks. If we don't have trial periods, where would we stand if we made a bad selection decision?

Answer

Depending on how many weeks' service have been completed when you realise someone isn't up to scratch then you could have to give a week's notice – and this will apply irrespective of whether a trial period is in force or not. The main point is to ask yourself how many times you've actually invoked trial periods over, say, the last five years.

Shorter trials

Question

Will we gain anything by shortening our trial periods from twelve to four weeks?

Answer

The period of nail biting is shorter, yes, but the fear factor is still there. The fact that the axe could fall sooner rather than later doesn't take the fear away.

Continental shifts

Question

Are continental shift patterns unpopular? We do a four on/four off pattern and we have both retention and recruitment problems with our skilled workforce.

Answer

Some people like continental shifts, some don't. The important thing is that you are sourcing the former category correctly. This comes down once again to your accessibility – stating in your ads what the shift patterns are.

Dirty conditions where the pay is average

Question

We are a traditional grey iron foundry and our problem is recruiting electricians. We always make a point of showing applicants round and most of them turn white when they see the conditions. Electricians, we find, are people who are looking for nice clean jobs in light industries. Our work is shift work and the rates we pay are roughly on a par with other foundries. Is this a case of just learning to live with our problems?

Answer

We are wondering about your accessibility. If your applicants are turning white when you show them round then they clearly don't realise the job is in a foundry. Is this made clear in your ads? If by your inaccessibility you're attracting the wrong kind of people (ie electricians who only want to work in clean conditions) then you're giving yourselves two major problems:

• you're wasting your time interviewing unsuitable applicants;

- you're convincing yourself you can't recruit. You're falling into the trap of a false logic – the electricians we interview only want clean jobs therefore all electricians only want clean jobs – which isn't true.

Somewhere out there, there are electricians who don't mind working shifts, who just want a fair day's pay for a fair day's work and who don't mind a bit of dust on their boots. By making yourself accessible to the market these are the kind of people you will be getting through to.

TRAINING

Applicants for apprenticeships not of the right calibre

Question

We can get plenty of applicants for apprenticeships but what bothers us is the standard – particularly in mathematics. Our shortfall in recruitment is because of this reason. Frankly we see no point at all in setting on youngsters in craft apprenticeships whose numeracy skills are inadequate. What's the answer?

Answer

You may not fall into this category but frequently we find that the firms who complain most about the standard of school leavers are firms who are recruiting 16 year olds. Again, we come back to the point that more gifted pupils stay on into sixth forms these days – hence the ones with the numeracy skills you are looking for may be coming available at 18 plus. We don't readily subscribe to the view that young people are worse in mathematics than they were 20 or 30 years ago. We can certainly remember firms grousing about school leavers with poor maths skills in the 60s.

Using ex-apprentices as skilled people on the cheap

Question

While accepting the broad point we do take exception to your case study (Nick, see page 119) because it resembles very closely what we have done with one of our own ex-apprentices, ie provided him with training and experience in areas of new technology which will greatly enhance his future prospects. As with Nick we are not paying this young man the rate we would expect to have to pay a highly experienced person in his/her 30s and 40s from outside the company and we feel this is being perfectly reasonable.

Given that we appear to have got this wrong can you please explain what we ought to be doing?

Answer

You haven't got anything wrong and we are sure your young man is as appreciative as Nick for the opportunity he has been given. The potential problem, though, lies in the future – when you fail to pick up that this young man you've invested all this money in training is now someone with highly sought-after skills – skills which command a much higher market rate that you are paying him. He will go and you will be the loser. It's a classic case of you can't beat the market. As you have probably gathered, what we are using Nick to illustrate is how firms, almost by omission, lose the people they've trained. It's a pity and they usually end up regretting it when it's too late.

Ex-apprentices being enticed away

Question

We are a firm who do apprentice training – and plenty of it. Our problem is we find ourselves training for the whole industrial estate – to the point where we're considering going round neighbouring firms and asking them how many people they intend to take off us in the next five years so we can plan our intakes! The firms we are talking about are all fairly small which means when they want to they have the flexibility to offer a few pounds more than we are paying. Is there anything we can do other than hope our neighbours don't have too many vacancies?

Answer

Yours is perhaps one of the most difficult retention situations. You are ringed in by predators and your only hopes are that:

- your people will stay with you because they want to – the feelgood factor;

- (as you say) your neighbours won't have too many vacancies.

Perhaps the only interesting point to consider is that your predators are small firms and, though you may not like the idea, contractual restraints may provide you with some answers, particularly if these firms compete with you for business. In your case a restraint could be inserted in the terms of any of your new apprentices to say that they mustn't, if they leave you, go and work for any firm within a five-mile radius (which would presumably cover your industrial estate). To make your strategy effective you must make it known to your predators that (a) these clauses have been inserted in your apprentices' contracts and that (b) you won't hesitate to use them. Can we guarantee you will be successful if you pursue a restraint such as this through the courts? No we can't and remember, the force of the restraint is in the threat rather than in its actual use. We say again this may not be to your liking and we would understand if you say 'no thank you'. Consult a solicitor or someone with HR training if you want to draft a restraint.

17

A Final Word

In arranging the topics in this book we have attempted to come full circle – from looking at the kinds of recruitment and retention difficulties which beset employers of skilled people at the present time and what can be done to help them, through to desperate remedies and back to the real long-term solution which lies in provision of the right levels of training.

In a perfect world we wouldn't have skills shortages but we are *not* living in a perfect world, in fact far from it. Even if we manage to get our skills training act right from now on we won't have enough skilled people to go round for many years to come. If we don't get our training act right, then we will be living with skills shortages forever – and that, sad as it seems, is a very real prospect.

A lot of the prescriptions we have put forward will be viewed as robbing Peter to pay Paul but, regrettable as it may be, we can't solve one firm's skills shortages without depriving someone else – not in the present circumstances. The beneficiaries, though, from the techniques we have described, will be those firms who succeed in giving skilled retention and recruitment the attention it needs, in short those who are prepared to work at it and there must be some justice in that.

METHODS

Like all practitioners we have arrived at the methods we use by building on experience – responding to situations; seeing what works and what doesn't; incorporating the lessons we learn into our body of know-how.

Though we have specialised in skills recruiting for many years we do not claim to have a monopoly on ideas about the subject. Indeed, what appears in this book should be viewed as an amalgam of best practice – a sort of state of the art incorporating techniques which companies have used and shared with us (our thanks to them).

Chiefly, though, we hope readers will find this practitioner base to our material reassuring. We have used the recruitment techniques we describe ourselves many, many times and with what, we are happy to say, has been a 95 per cent plus success rate. And when firms come along to us saying this or that hasn't worked, the reason we usually find is that they have followed the advice piecemeal. They have picked out bits they like the sound of or bits they find easy and disregarded something quite fundamental.

Our success rate serves to demonstrate just how many 'can't recruit' situations are resolvable. In other words, in less than 5 per cent of cases only have we had to entertain the kind of prescriptions we have put under the heading of 'desperate measures'. Firms who are at the moment doing such things as recruiting out of area should take a special note of this. Before you go any further try revisiting your own backyard, this time using the right methods.

Have we tried using these methods to recruit people in other scarce skills categories?

The answer is yes. With some modifications and refinements we have used the same sort of approach to recruit odd specialists and technical people such as design engineers. Again, on the whole, the combination of accessibility, availability and application works.

DEVELOPING RETENTION AND RECRUITMENT TECHNIQUES

This is not a static subject but one in which new ideas are coming on the scene all the time. Coupled with which the market and its behaviour is changing constantly. The ultra-wariness with which skilled people are viewing the job market today is, for example, a relatively recent development.

You will learn as you go on to develop the techniques you are using: to update them and to customise them to your own particular circumstances. What we have tried to do in this book is to give you the framework and to leave the frills for you to insert. For instance, we occasionally get people saying to us that our step-in off the street open sessions are far too stark for their liking. Our answer is that this is, in part, intentional because busy recruiters in a hurry will think twice about using anything which is unwieldy and complex to set up – the simplicity or starkness is in this respect important. Also, any embellishing on the basic is, we feel, best left to you and a lot will depend on the resources you have available, eg staff to receive applicants, serve them with drinks and so on.

Another facet to customising techniques is where you are trying to recruit people with really scarce skills such as special-ised, unusual trades which are found just in one industry. Here, very often, you will find yourself in 'choice of one' situations and that is if you are lucky. What you need to be prepared for is to roll all your sourcing and selecting into one exercise, eg applicant walks in off street; applicant is given preliminary interview on the spot by HR officer; applicant is introduced to line manager; applicant (if suitable) leaves with job offer. Asking some highly sought-after candidate to come back when you've got a bit more time certainly isn't recommended.

Sometimes you won't know in advance that the skills you are trying to source fit into this ultra-scarce category. You may have a new job – new to you, that is – for example associated with a new process or a new piece of machinery. You may, on the other hand, be replacing someone who has been with you for a long time. Many years have passed since you last tried to recruit someone with this particular blend of skills and in all of these situations you will need to retain a certain amount of *flexibility* – to be ready, in other words, to spring into a scarce skills recruiting mode if it becomes necessary. This becomes very much a case of being on your toes and keeping your wits about you.

Where you are recruiting people regularly within a certain skills category you will rapidly start to build up a feel for what your local market has to offer if it is sourced properly. You will start to know what sort of response to expect and how to enhance that response (by tweaking and twiddling the formulas). Don't be afraid to experiment.

STRUCTURING SOLUTIONS TO SKILLS SHORTAGES

Structuring your approach to skills shortages – taking it a step at a time – is important because there is a learning curve to follow. For example, if you source your local area properly, by good, clear, accessible advertising backed up with lots of availability, you will soon learn whether you are dealing with a pay problem or whether you are trying to source skills which are genuinely scarce. You can then proceed accordingly. You can hike up your pay if this is what is called for. You can take stock of genuine scarcity of skills. Hopefully, of course, you won't have to do either of these things because your skills sourcing will have worked.

In contrast if you move straight from poor sourcing/poor response to putting in a big pay increase and this still doesn't ease your recruiting difficulties (remember Gripnuts) then you still won't know what's at fault. Was it:

- your sourcing?

- your pay (the increase wasn't enough)?

In short, you are no further advanced in knowing what to do about your situation. One thing is certain though – there's no going back on your pay increase.

PUTTING IT INTO PRACTICE

Everything you have read in this book about skills recruiting can be put into practice straight away. You may need to install a direct phone line (if you don't happen to have one already) but apart from that and if you need to get on with filling skilled vacancies then there is nothing to stop you starting today.

One piece of advice we would offer to you, however, is to try at the outset to dispose of any preconceived ideas you may have on where you are going wrong with your skilled retention and recruitment. Most practitioners we meet do have preconceived ideas but on the whole we find these don't help or they tend to fog the real issues.

A few years ago a company asked us to carry out a recruitment assignment for them. This company happened to be located in a new town – an area which had a high concentration of high-tech manufacturing plants – offshoots, in many cases, of large multinationals. Our client, in contrast, operated in a very basic and unglamorous industry.

The problem here was recruitment of maintenance electricians. The company urgently needed to replace two leavers and, up to the point of our involvement, they had restricted their sourcing to registering their two vacancies with the local Job Centre. The response so far had been precisely nil.

Why hadn't they advertised? The reason given was quite interesting. The company had noticed that a lot of their high-tech neighbours also had vacancies for maintenance electricians and were regularly putting huge quarter or half-page display advertisements in the local evening paper. It was rumoured furthermore that some of these companies were paying very high wages: 'If *they* can't recruit what chance do we stand?' was the way our client saw its predicament. The scene was therefore set for the company to start reassessing its rates of pay.

We treated this recruitment assignment in precisely the same way as we would treat any other recruitment assignment. We advertised under the company's name and gave applicants the choice of phoning in or attending an open session – or writing in if they preferred. The response was not tremendous but sufficient for our client to fill both vacancies.

The moral to this tale is not to let yourself be led by random impressions or things you have heard. In particular the fact that someone else is having recruitment problems is best ignored. The someone elses in question could well be using poor sourcing methods and for evidence don't look at the size or the snazziness of their ads but focus in instead on the little tailpieces at the bottom which tell interested parties how to apply. If these lack availability then it's not surprising they can't recruit. Also if the big snazzy ads keep appearing time and time again then the diminishing return effect sets in ('it's them again!').

Another piece of advice is not to give up if, the first time you use our skill sourcing techniques, they don't work. Don't, whatever you do, go back to what you did before or, worse still, give up completely. Learn instead to read the signs. Listen to what the market you have now properly sourced is telling you. If necessary retrace your steps and begin again.

A company we had some dealings with not long ago had formed the opinion that its rates of pay were way below the market level. We were less sure but suggested that the best way to test the hypothesis was by putting it to the market, ie carrying out a sourcing exercise with maximum accessibility and availability. The company ran an ad in the local evening paper. The rate of pay didn't appear in the ad but applicants had the facility to discuss this over the phone.

In the event this sourcing exercise proved the company right. The applicants who phoned in (the suitable ones) were all looking for higher rates than the company paid. As a result the company decided to hike up its pay scales for skilled grades quite substantially. Next they recontacted some of the applicants they had heard from previously. Several weeks had lapsed and without exception all these people had now got themselves fixed up. The company then went back to readvertising in a very traditional format. Applicants were asked to write in or send a CV. This time there was no facility to ring in and talk about pay. The response was disappointing, perhaps predictably.

'What happened to your accessibility and availability?' was the first question we asked them. 'Oh, that didn't work,' they said, 'there was no point in trying it again'.

The object lesson here is that the 3As are not disposable and the relative success of any skilled recruiting you do depends always on the consistency with which you use these principles. On its own hiking up pay doesn't advance you very far unless you can also:

- get it across to the people you are trying to recruit that your rates are good – or make it easy for them to find out.

- still provide for busy people working long and/or awkward hours.

Index